A History of the Great Western Railway
1. Consolidation, 1923–29

A History of the Great Western Railway
1. Consolidation, 1923-29

Peter Semmens, M.A., C.Chem., F.R.S.C., M.B.C.S., M.C.I.T.

London
GEORGE ALLEN & UNWIN
Boston   Sydney

First published in 1985
Reprinted 1986, 1987, 1988
Reprinted 1990 by Studio Editions Ltd. by
arrangement with George Allen & Unwin.

Studio Editions Ltd.
Princess House, 50 Eastcastle Street,
London W1N 7 AP, England

Printed in Great Britain by Biddles Ltd.
Guildford, Surrey.

Contents

List of Illustrations and Tables

Tables

Foreword

(From the Speech of Sir Robert Horne at the General Meeting of the Great Western Railway Company, 27 February 1935.)

'On the 31st day of August, 1835, the Great Western Railway Company was incorporated. This great organisation, of which those assembled here today are the modern representatives, is therefore within six months of completing a public service extending over the most remarkable century of human progress known to history. During this epoch the Company has experienced periods of vicissitude as well as of good fortune; of acute anxiety as well as serene confidence; of exasperating failure as well as encouraging success; but through all those times, good and ill, the reputation of the Railway has stood high in popular favour and we are today the heirs of a system which absorbs our interest and commands our loyalty.'

Reproduced from the Centenary Brochure of the Great Western Railway.

I
The Heritage

Alone of the Big Four railways of the grouping era the Great Western Railway consisted primarily of a single existing company. Not for Paddington or Swindon were there the managerial and engineering traumas resulting from the amalgamation of near-equal partners, such as the Midland and North-Western within the LMS. Indeed, by the time our railways were nationalised in 1948, the Great Western Railway could boast an unbroken management tradition stretching back no less than 112 years to the passing of their first Act of Parliament in 1835. The six constituent companies that combined with the GWR in 1923 contributed just under a quarter to the capital assets of the new company but less than 15 per cent of the net revenue. Some of the constituents were appreciable concerns in their own right, but their effects on the future policies and fortunes of the enlarged GWR were relatively small. To set the scene on our study we must thus initially concentrate on the GWR's own heritage.

The Great Western Railway was conceived to link London and Bristol, the latter being the second city of the kingdom into the 1820s. As a port facing the New World, its maritime activities were pre-eminent, as still recalled by the phrase 'All ship-shape and Bristol fashion'. Business circles there had long sought a better connection with the capital, and even before the opening of the Stockton & Darlington Railway in 1825 a prospectus was issued for a line from Bristol to London. However, it was not until the autumn of 1832 that a meeting of four influential Bristol businessmen really got the project under way. An enlarged committee commissioned a survey of the proposed route, and in the light of this there was the vital public meeting in the Guildhall at Bristol in July 1833, which firmly resolved that 'a Company should be formed for establishment of Railway Communication between Bristol and London . . .'. Separate committees were formed in Bristol and London, a move clearly indicative of the poor communications that then existed between these two centres. Less than three weeks later the title 'Great Western Railway' was adopted for the proposed company, and a prospectus was issued to raise £3m, with an initial 5 per cent call on each share.

Given this parentage, the standing of the company was in little doubt in the area it was intended to serve, but much of its 'style' was to derive from its engineer, Isambard Kingdom Brunel, who was a mere twenty-seven years of age when appointed in March 1833. The 'Little Giant', as he was to become known, had nevertheless already performed great personal feats during the construction of his father's Thames Tunnel, and was the winner of the competition to design the Clifton Suspension Bridge. He was to expend great energy over the following few years, speeding across the countryside in his specially-built carriage, nicknamed the 'Flying Hearse', during the construction of the railway. Over and above this, however, he showed a boldness of approach with the engineering of the line that was to become his hallmark in later years.

Not for Brunel and the GWR was that gauge of track which had crept out from the collieries on to the main lines in the north. In the dozen years since George Stephenson had adopted a distance of 4ft 8in between the rails for the Stockton & Darlington, the potential for a railway based on a wider track had become clear to Brunel, and so he adopted the broad gauge of 7ft 0¼in. Where the quarter-inch came from is still a mystery, although the corresponding odd half-inch that was to characterise the standard-gauge of 4ft 8½in until recent years was provided to increase the clearance between flanges and check-rails on points and crossings. Today's Imperial equivalent of the British standard of 1432mm is 4ft 8⅜in, the eighth of an inch disappearing in the interests of better bogie stability at today's high speeds.

Together with the adoption of the broad gauge, Brunel's main line from London to Bristol was characterised by the use of the baulk road, with its longitudinal timbers supporting the bridge rails for their full length, and its superb layout. Structures like the Maidenhead Bridge across the Thames, and the tunnels at Box, were immense by the standards of their day. The bridge, doubled in the 1880s, now carries today's High Speed Trains at 125 mph, while it is only the aerodynamic effects in the tunnel which restrict their speed at that point to a mere ninety. For much of the distance Brunel fixed the maximum gradient at a mere eight feet to the mile, and as a result the line was known,

1. The Great Western Railway's 'coat of arms', consisting of those of the cities of London and Bristol. This was the form used from the mid-1920s onwards. Prior to that the shields had been enclosed in a 'garter' device. In neither form was it registered by the College of Arms, which was a comparable state of affairs with most other British railway companies.

from the 1840s onwards, for its high-speed running. In 1848 Daniel Gooch was able to refer to the fact that the morning express from Paddington was '. . . in the constant practice of running the 53 miles to Didcot, without stopping, in 48 to 50 minutes . . .'. Since the advent of the High Speed Train, Brunel's alignment has permitted consistently fast running over long distances, culminating in the establishment of the latest world record of 112.7 mph from Paddington to Bristol in 1984. In 1975 the APT–E had set up a new British railway speed record of 152 mph utilising part of the same stretch and could undoubtedly have gone faster still had not the rising air temperature limited the power available from its gas turbines.

The first section of the GWR to be opened to the public was between London and Maidenhead on 2 June 1838, but it was not until the opening of the stretch between Chippenham and Bath on 30 June 1841 that the line was complete throughout from London to Bristol. Notwithstanding the financial over-runs, by this time the potential of the enterprise had been realised, and extensions to the broad gauge as well as the construction of various branches were in hand or under active consideration.

This was of course the period of the 'railway mania', and with the rapid growth of our railway system, only four years were to elapse before the opening skirmishes of the gauge war occurred. Government took a hand in the matter, and in spite of the proven superiority of the broad gauge locomotive performance, the Gauge Act effectively put an end to the development of Brunel's system away from the areas already covered by the GWR and its allies. They were forced to lay their first narrow-gauge tracks, as they termed them, in the mid-1850s, and a decade later saw Brunel's legacy at its zenith. By then 1,040 miles of broad gauge track, supplemented by 387 miles of mixed-gauge, stretched from London to Weymouth, Penzance, Milford Haven and Wolverhampton, with more than thirty breaks of gauge occurring on the periphery where they caused endless trouble to passengers and freight alike.

For the next quarter century, having weathered a difficult financial period in the mid-1860s under the chairmanship of Daniel Gooch, much of the GWR's resources had inevitably to be directed towards the ultimate conversion of the whole system to the narrow gauge, hereinafter to be referred to as 'standard'. However, even in its act of dying, the broad gauge was the cause of Herculean efforts. The first major scheme was in South Wales where 240 miles were converted in May 1872, but the final and greatest feat was the alteration of 171 miles west of Exeter during a single weekend in May 1892. So Brunel's broad gauge passed away, mourned by many and of sufficient national significance to be the subject of a poem and cartoon in Punch.

With the railway system of the British Isles building up to the zenith of its influence and prosperity in the first decade of the twentieth century, the GWR, with the traumas of the gauge conversion behind it, was quick to shake off the moribund shackles that had fettered it for the previous thirty years. In the spring of 1892 the first British train with vestibule connections throughout was introduced on the Birkenhead line, to be followed in the next year by others running to Torbay and Penzance. Dean's elegant outside-framed locomotives were capable of giving a good account of themselves, and in 1904, 'City of Truro', gained immortality on the descent of Wellington Bank with an Ocean Mail special from Plymouth to Paddington. While the speed of 100 mph reached on that occasion constituted a world record, so far ahead was it of the time that the full details were not released by the GWR until 1922.

Fine though these double-framed locomotives were, their detailed design was such that they could not be enlarged to meet the demands being made on the motive power to haul heavier and faster trains during Edwardian times. In 1902, however, Dean was succeeded as Locomotive and Carriage Superintendent at Swindon by Churchward, and under his direction the whole course of locomotive engineering in this country took a major leap forward. So ahead of the time was his thinking that as late as 1925 the LNER was indulging in 'industrial espionage' to determine the details of GWR locomotive valve gears, while one of the standard designs outlined by Churchward did not even appear until 1951, three years after nationalisation.

Partly as a result of the stagnation caused by the long-awaited demise of the broad gauge, the initials GWR were, by the turn of the century, often used to refer to the Great *Way* Round. While the opening of the Severn Tunnel in 1886 had markedly shortened the route from London to South Wales, it was not until 1903 that the line from Wootton Bassett to Patchway cut a further ten miles off the distance. The new line was laid out for high-speed running throughout in contrast to the older route which had to thread the junctions at Bristol and the curves at Bath. In the summer of 1906 the West of England route via Westbury was opened, fulfilling an ambition first authorised by Parliament in 1848. No longer was it necessary for the trains to the West Country resorts to be routed via Bristol, and the 'Cornish Riviera Express' had twenty miles cut off its world record non-stop run from Paddington to Plymouth. The last of the major shortcuts, taking 18½ miles off the distance from Paddington to Birmingham, was not opened until 1910 and shared part of the route with the Great Central. This particular line seems to have been used to capacity in World War I as a Traders Season Ticket issued to an employee of the Vickers armament firm in 1918 is overstamped on the cover 'Not Valid via Bicester'.

Not all these new lines served the routes that radiated from London. In July 1908 the GWR's own route was opened from Birmingham to Cheltenham, enabling it to run through expresses to the West of England using its own lines below the western scarp of the Cotswolds and those over which they had running powers. In addition to these particular large-scale cut-offs,

there was widespread construction of shorter lengths of new line elsewhere to provide more competitive services or simply to meet the growing transport demands of the mother country on whose Empire the sun never set.

It was the assassin's bullets in Sarajevo in 1914 that were to take Britain over the top of the hill in the four years of hostilities that were to follow, with the flower of her manhood killed in the trenches of the Western Front and elsewhere, while the railways strove to keep the fighting machine supplied with the increasingly complicated munitions of war. More than 2,400 of the GWR's staff were to die in the armed forces during the conflict. In order to coordinate the transport services of the country during the hostilities, all the railways had been placed under government control. With the dawning of peace it became apparent that there were advantages in continuing something more akin to the wartime arrangements rather than once again reverting to the separate railway companies numbering over one hundred that still existed. After toying with the possibilities of nationalisation, Parliament finally passed the Railways Act of 1921, which decreed that there would be four major railway groups, each serving predominantly a single part of the country. In three of the cases the formation of these groups came about by the amalgamation of several partners of near-equal size. In the case of the GWR, the other constituent and subsidiary companies did no more than increase its capital by 40 per cent, and we will be discussing their contribution to the new company in the next chapter. It is thus appropriate to conclude this account of the GWR's heritage by reviewing the system as it existed in the early 1920s.

According to the Ministry of Transport returns, in the month of December 1921 the Great Western handled 7.2m passengers, excluding season ticket holders, its nearest rivals amongst

2. The last days of the broad gauge. A down train approaches Teignmouth along the sea wall in 1892. Every alternate transom has been cut ready for the narrowing of the gauge that took place on 20–23 May 1892.

the main-line railway companies being the MR and LNWR, both of which exceeded the 7.1m mark. In the same month the GWR hauled 4.2m tons of revenue freight, again putting it in pride of place on the national league table over the MR, NER and LNWR which filled the next three places. When it came to ton-miles, however, the longer hauls of the MR gave it a 1 per cent edge on the GWR, but after them the NER could only manage three-quarters of their figure.

The total route mileage owned by the GWR at the end of 1920 was almost exactly 3,000, including those lines it leased, as well as its share of jointly owned lines. Heading the list were the 427¾ route miles from London to Penzance via Bristol and via Frome, followed by Swindon to Fishguard, and Didcot to Chester. Altogether there were 1,334 miles of 'Main and Principal Lines'. In nearly every case in England (as distinct from Wales), there was a greater mileage of 'Minor and Branch Lines' associated with each, giving a total under this heading of 1,318. Just over eighty-one miles of new railway had been authorised but not opened, of which only about a quarter were actually under construction at the end of 1920.

3. 4–6–0 no 2925 'Saint Martin'. This locomotive was built in 1907 and in 1924 was reconstructed as the prototype of the Hall class mixed-traffic locomotives with 6 ft diameter driving wheels.

H. C. Casserley

Since the appointment of Daniel Gooch as the first Locomotive Superintendent in 1837, there had been only four holders of this office up to the beginning of 1922, although that year was to see Churchward retiring in favour of Collett. By this time the locomotive stock of the GWR totalled just over 3,100. The list in the annual report was headed by the solitary Pacific, 'The Great Bear', the building of which in 1908 had preceded the construction of the next British locomotive with this wheel arrangement by no less than fourteen years. Most numerous amongst the other wheel arrangements were the 0–6–0s, some 1,100 tank locomotives of this configuration being in service, in addition to 400 of the tender variety. The combined total serves

as a reminder that this particular wheel arrangement was the most popular of any throughout the steam era in this country. These locomotives were supplemented by the steam rail motors and the GWR's half-share of the electric rolling stock of the Hammersmith & City Railway. To conclude the motive-power line-up, there were 100 horses on the strength. These were those used for shunting purposes, over and above the 2,800 for road vehicles.

Churchward's range of locomotives was spearheaded by his 4–6–0 express passenger designs and the 2–8–0 heavy freight locomotives. His thinking had first emerged with the twin-cylinder 4–6–0 no. 100 which appeared in 1902, and after experimenting with the Atlantic wheel arrangement, the original layout became firmly established as the standard for all the GWR's subsequent express passenger locomo-

18

4. A Barnum 2–4–0 no 3219 on a horsebox special in August 1926. This locomotive was built in 1889 and superheated in 1928 before being withdrawn in 1935.

tives. As was customary for such locomotives on the GWR, they were named, and became known generally as the Saint class. Even the 'Great Bear' Pacific, already referred to, ultimately shed its trailing axle to become a 4–6–0. That was a four-cylinder locomotive, however, based on the Star 4–6–0s of 1907 which had been preceded by the four-cylinder 'North Star' built with the Atlantic wheel arrangement to give a more direct comparison with the three de Glehn compounds that the GWR had imported from France. By early in 1923 there were 73 four-cylinder Stars and 77 two-cylinder Saints in service. With their coned superheated boilers the Stars had shown themselves fully capable of fulfilling the designer's requirement to produce a drawbar pull of two tons at 70 mph, corresponding to a drawbar-horsepower of 835. This enabled them to give a good account of themselves on the West of England expresses, both when running at high speeds on the easier grades or slogging up the South Devon banks west of

5. Aberdare 2–6–0 no 2662 on an up coal train on the GWR main line in January 1927. In 1902 this particular locomotive was the first to appear in standard form with the Swindon no 4 coned boiler. It was one of the last survivors of the class, not being withdrawn until July 1948.

M. W. Earley Collection, National Railway Museum, York

Newton Abbot. In 1910, trials had been carried out between the LNWR Experiments and the GWR Stars which showed the latter's superiority, and even when Crewe subsequently produced their four-cylinder Claughtons many of the vital design points were missed.

Like any main-line railway of its day, the majority of the GWR's income came from freight, and Churchward introduced the 2–8–0 wheel arrangement into the country in 1903, the locomotive and its subsequent developments sharing a standard boiler design with the Saints and Stars. Whereas the Stars were to be superseded as the GWR's top link express passenger locomotives as early as 1923, Churchward's 2–8–0 freight locomotives continued to be constructed with only minor changes right through until 1942. The demands of World War II required the adoption of a national standard that had a wider route availability than locomotives that took full advantage of the Brunel loading-gauge. Even so the last of them was not withdrawn until 1965, while no. 2818, the member of the class preserved at the National Railway

Museum, ran no less than 1,584,890 miles in service. As with Churchward's passenger locomotives, his 2–8–0s were also involved in exchange trials. The first of these was in 1921 on the North British Railway in Scotland. On the second occasion, over a quarter of a century later, in the course of hauling the loose-coupled freights out of the murky depths of the Severn Tunnel and trundling them along the main line to Acton, it was a Churchward 2–8–0 that achieved the highest thermal efficiency of any of the fourteen different classes of locomotive involved in the post-nationalisation locomotive exchange trials of 1948.

Great Western locomotives were also noted for their handsome appearance, their most outstanding visual adornment probably being their copper-capped chimneys, supplemented by the enormous brass-covered domes of the parallel-boilered locomotives, setting off the Brunswick green livery lined out with orange and black. The tapered-boiler Churchward locomotives combined a top-feed arrangement with a brass casing round the safety valves in the middle of the barrel, giving them a distinctive appearance. The rigours of World War I had, however, their effect on such splendour, an unlined green paint scheme finally being adopted, which even obscured the brass and copper-work, so that at grouping in 1923 the general appearance of GWR trains was far more sombre than it had been in their Edwardian heyday. The traditional chocolate and cream livery of the coaching stock had also given way to a dark lake in 1908.

The success of Churchward's locomotives was due not only to the carefully thought-out standardisation programme, but also to the adoption and development of various technical improvements. Documents in the archives at the National Railway Museum show how information was gathered in to Swindon from all over the world, and mention has already been made of the purchase of three French locomotives. Even after the basic ideas had been laid down, developments such as superheating, taper boilers and top feed were introduced over the years that followed, while, at the same time, Swindon's techniques and standards of workmanship were unsurpassed. Churchward's valve gears were nearly robust enough to move the locomotive, let alone the piston valves, and, even at the end of the steam era, the evenness and sharpness of the exhaust beats of GWR locomotives was outstanding. With the tradition of craftsmanship in the works went a similar attention to detail out on the road. Every GWR fireman was trained to lift the flap into the open firehole door each time before turning away to refill his shovel. This meant he then had to give another quick jerk to the chain to get it out of the way before he could fling the next shovelful of coal on to the incandescent fire, involving a dozen extra operations every mile compared with the practice on other railways. The fire used traditionally to be built up into the shape of a haycock, with a covering of unburnt slack just inside the firehole door to cut down the effect of the heat on the fireman. From the drivers' point of view the controls were well arranged, and so precise was the driver's ability to set the regulator opening exactly as required that trains could be seen moving out of Paddington with the driver's hands nowhere near the handle, so confident was he that the locomotive would not suddenly slip.

At the end of 1920 the GWR owned some 5,500 passenger carriages and 80,000 merchandise and mineral vehicles, but it must not be overlooked that most of the country's coal traffic was at that time hauled in private-owners' wagons. There were just over 8,000 service vehicles, more than half of them being for the transport of locomotive coal.

Taken overall, the GWR's coaching stock

Lens of Sutton

6. One of Churchward's 2–8–0 freight locomotives, no 2881, in immaculate ex-works condition. The massive brackets that provided rigidity between the boiler and slide bars on this class are very apparent.

when grouping took place does not seem to have been as advanced in design as in its motive power. Indeed more coaches were put into service in the ten years from 1845 than during the whole of Churchward's reign at Swindon. Many of Dean's clerestory vehicles were still in service in 1922, and were to remain in operation for a further two decades. Their construction had been succeeded by the revolutionary Dreadnought coaching stock which first appeared in

1904, their seventy-foot length and 9ft 6in width taking full advantage of the generous GWR loading-gauge. They were not too well received by the travelling public, however, and were followed by other designs in 1906 and 1907. It was the 'toplight' stock, introduced in the latter year, that was to become the standard for new construction right through to the 1920s. The name is derived from the oblong windows of hammered glass set above the main windows to improve the level of interior illumination. The glass panes along the side of the clerestories were undoubtedly also intended for the same pur-

7. A three-car train of Great Western & Metropolitan electric stock at Addison Road station, Kensington in August 1933.

pose, although they would have been far less easily kept clean. Indeed, when one looks at the large number of clerestory coaches round the world that were not provided with clear or frosted glass in these locations, one is led to the conclusion that the constructional complications of this particular roof-line were dictated by other reasons. As late as 1925 only about a quarter of the GWR coaches were electrically lit, and the nineteenth-century alternative was gas, which resulted in a considerable ventilation problem. The clerestory roof not only provided extra height to accommodate the heated air and products of combustion, but ventilators could readily be provided along their sides.

Another feature of the GWR passenger scene during the first quarter of the twentieth-century was the extensive use of the steam rail-motor, although by the advent of grouping the change-over to auto-train operation using locomotives and specially equipped coaches was well under way. Many of the self-contained rail-motors had actually already been converted to auto-trailers by the 1920s, although in their self-propelled form some were to remain in service until 1935.

Railways, however, comprise much more than coloured lines on maps or locomotives striding across the countryside at the head of passenger and freight trains. There are terminal facilities to be provided, and it is of course the passenger stations and their facilities that are most likely to impress themselves on the public's consciousness. From the beginning, the original GWR London to Bristol line was noted for its two terminal stations: Paddington and Temple Meads. Brunel had had a hand in both, and it is fitting that the present-day resurgence of British Rail's pride in its architectural heritage should be marked by the unveiling of a statue to the designer at Paddington, commissioned by a Bristol building society. The 1854 train-shed at Paddington was in 1922 nearing the end of an extensive renewal programme, which followed the completion of the new fourth span in 1916.

23

In spite of bomb damage during World War II, the station today sees the comings and goings of High Speed Trains, diesel locomotives and multiple-units with a frequency that would have been thought astounding not so many years ago. 'The Lawn' beyond the buffer stops has been the site of so many farewells and reunions over more than a century and a quarter, while millions have queued patiently there for the trains to take them on holiday or evacuate them to the country areas to the west of the war-threatened capital. The alteration of Temple Meads into a through station, rather than a terminus, removed much of the operational importance of Brunel's original train-shed there, with its wooden-beamed roof, and for several years now it has been bereft of rails. The cooperation of British Railways and the preservation trust will now ensure the future of this totally different example of Brunel's architecture.

It is difficult to do justice to all the salient features of Great Western architecture in such a brief summary as this, but whether it was a small country station or a massive main-line viaduct, the GWR's own characteristic signature could be noted. While Brunel's hand could be seen at places like Pangbourne, the introduction of steam rail-motors in the 1900s had resulted in the widespread construction of halts provided with highly characteristic small 'pagodas'. There were in 1922 still some of Brunel's timber viaducts in service, although many had already been replaced to permit the passage of heavier locomotives.

Railways in this country have long been in the hotel business, although in recent years the speed-up in train travel, coupled with our changed styles of living, rendered them a less valuable asset to our present-day impecunious railway organisation, and they were sold off in 1983. Indeed one of the first tasks that faced the Stockton & Darlington Railway after the success

of the opening day in September 1825 was the provision of hotel accommodation for their would-be passengers. It is thus no surprise that by the 1920s the Great Western Railway was operating a chain of hotels stretching from London to St Ives and Fishguard. At Paddington the Great Western Royal Hotel actually forms the frontage of the station and has its own entrance direct from 'The Lawn'. Opened by the Prince Consort in 1854, two weeks after the present station came into full operation, the hotel had always been one of the best in London. Originally built by some of the directors and operated as a separate company, it was taken over by the railway in 1896 and extensively modernised by the standards of the day. By 1907 lifts and electric light had been installed, while guests could send messages by pneumatic tube to the kitchen or the telegraph office from their rooms.

Altogether there were eight hotels owned by the GWR in 1922. Two were in Wales at Fishguard and Neyland, while the remaining five were situated in the West of England. The 'George & Railway' at Bristol was located comparatively close to the Portishead Hotel, while the remaining three were at Taunton, Plymouth and St Ives.

The hotels were by no means the only property owned by the GWR. Their 1922 returns showed the ownership of the following areas of land and houses:

	Acres
Agricultural land	2379
Urban and suburban land	1453

	Houses
Labouring class dwellings	170
Houses and cottages for company's Servants	1459
Other houses and cottages	1135

8. Steam railmotor no 84 on the GWR main line near Sonning in May 1925. This unit had been built in 1907 and in 1930 it was converted to auto trailer no 183.

All railways have been landowners, if only as a result of the initial purchase of packages of land left over from that actually needed for the building of the line. Elsewhere the need to accommodate key employees in rural areas resulted in the railways building houses for their staff in addition to the country stations of which the stationmaster's house traditionally formed an adjunct. Some of these buildings are still with us, one of the most notable being the stone-built house on the north side of the line at Steventon, still visible from an InterCity 125 unit as it hurtles through the now-demolished station at full speed. For those who might wonder at the standard of architecture provided for such a purpose, the building was originally constructed by Brunel for the Superintendent of Line. It was at Swindon, however, where the Great Western not only built its main locomotive works, but subsequently its carriage and wagon works as well. Right from the start it was necessary to provide accommodation for some of their workers, the first 300 cottages forming the nucleus of the New Town of Swindon. In recent years much of this pioneer housing has been very effectively restored to provide modern standards for those living there. This is a most welcome revival, particularly since, in these difficult times for the railways, the degree of involvement by British Rail Engineering Ltd in town affairs is inevitably much less than it was, even as late as the 1920s under the paternalism of the GWR. The local authority's interest in railways, long after this period, is exemplified by the opening of the Great Western Railway Museum in 1962, the exhibits being on loan from the National Collection which at that time came under the care of the BTC Curator of Historical Relics.

Railways the world over have become involved in the need to bring passengers and freight on to their systems, although in many

British Rail Western Region

9. The SS 'St Patrick' at speed. This was the first GW vessel of this name, dating from 1906 and operated mainly on the South-Wales-Southern Ireland services. She was replaced by a second ship of the same name in 1930.

cases the resulting feeder services subsequently become profitable operations in their own right. Like many railways that served those ports on the coasts of Britain that faced the short sea crossings to Ireland and the Continent, the Great Western Railway was in 1923 involved with its own shipping services. We will be discussing the ports themselves in Chapter IV, but at the time of the grouping the GWR owned nine 'steamboats' of over 250 tons net, and a similar number of smaller ones. The oldest was the 'Pembroke' of 1880 while the 'Waterford' was the most modern, dating from 1912. The 'Pembroke' served with the GWR for no less than forty-five years, initially on the Irish routes, but spending her last nine on the Channel Island services out of Weymouth. Starting life as a paddle steamer, she was given twin screws in 1896, and converted into a cargo vessel in 1916. The youngest ship in the GWR fleet in 1922 was the 'Water-

ford', actually built to replace the 'Pembroke'. It was originally proposed to name her 'Great Britain' after Brunel's pioneer vessel, now returned from dereliction to be restored and preserved in the dock at Bristol where she was built. In 1912 another vessel carried the name, and this unfortunately prevented the GWR from using it. The three largest and most powerful vessels in GWR's fleet at the time of the grouping were the 'St Andrew', the 'St David' and the 'St Patrick', the first dating from 1908 and the others being two years older.

The Great Western steamers provided services between South Wales and Ireland as well as from Weymouth to the Channel Isles. There was a considerable degree of integration between the two operations, with some of the vessels switching from the Irish Sea to the English Channel every summer. Certain of the ships were involved in various incidents during World War I. 'Pembroke' was fired on by a U-boat in 1916. Earlier than this, however, another of the GWR ships had actually been

26

10. 'Reindeer', one of the Great Western's pre-grouping steamers used on the Channel Island services, enters St Peterport harbour in Guernsey in August 1924. She was built in 1897.

sunk in Scapa Flow by getting herself impaled on a warship after her anchor had dragged. The 'Ibex', built in 1891, was still in service at the time of the grouping and had had an extremely chequered career. In January 1900 she struck a reef approaching Guernsey and sank with the loss of two lives. She was salvaged and returned to service just over fifteen months later. During World War I she was attacked three times by German U-boats, one of which she sank by gunfire. A brass plate recording her wartime services was subsequently mounted at the head of the saloon staircase until she was broken up in 1926.

It was not only by sea that the GWR operated feeder services to its railway stations; they became the first railway operators of 'road motors' in 1903 when one of the five vehicles they had ordered entered service between Helston and the Lizard. A second route from Penzance to Marazion soon followed. By the early 1920s, however, their passenger road operations were declining. A fleet of 130 road motors and omnibuses in 1919 had shrunk to 97 by 1923. This was in no way a reflection on the reliability of the new form of transport, as during the same period their fleet of road motors for goods and parcels rose from 121 to 392, while the horse-drawn vehicles similarly increased in numbers from 3,754 to 3,974. There was, surprisingly, a marked fall in the number of horses owned by the company, from 3,120 in 1919 to only 2,606 in 1923, probably indicating that the motor vehicles were handling the larger and heavier jobs, while the constituent and subsidiary companies undoubtedly contributed vehicle pools to the post-grouping GWR.

It was not only necessary to provide the actual feeder services to the railways, but passengers had to be encouraged to make the journey or rather to travel over a particular railway. The GWR held a unique position in the publicity field throughout its entire existence. Their earliest known pictorial poster (for the Ascot Races) dated from 1897, and within a few years they had coined one of the longest-lasting and most widely-known tourist slogans ever created – 'The Cornish Riviera'. The whole idea was

27

worked out in great depth with the classic poster from the late 1900s comparing the mirror-image similarities of Cornwall and Italy, complete with a Cornish girl in a folk costume that no Cousin Jenny would ever recognise! Not only does the name 'Cornish Riviera' still grace the principal daily HST workings between Paddington and Penzance, but the National Railway Museum sells thousands of postcards each year depicting the original plaque. To be fair, not all the publicity linkings between parts of Britain and their foreign equivalents caught on. How many of us would immediately recognise the 'Welsh Tyrol', which is depicted in one of the exhibits at the Swindon Museum illustrating the Snowdon area? Although perhaps the early 1920s found railway posters pictorially at a low ebb, there is no doubt that much of the Great Western's hold on public affection resulted from its publicity approach.

No organisation, however technically advanced, is a viable concern without the staff that operate it. In March 1921 (the last time prior to 1923 when there was a separate count) the total number of employees of all grades on the GWR was no less than 92,000, an almost unbelievable figure compared with the total of 161,000 for the whole of British Railways (including British Rail Engineering Limited) at the end of 1982. From the board of nineteen directors down to the porters and permanent-way labourers, there was the greatest possible stress on *esprit de corps*. The *Great Western Railway Magazine* was published for the staff and sold tens of thousands of copies every month. Much of each issue was devoted to news concerning the staff, including reports on social gatherings as well as discussion of safety and other operational matters. In the first three monthly issues for 1921 there are accounts of no less than twelve dinners or other similar get-togethers by groups of the staff throughout the system. The early 1920s were, of course, a period when the comradeship of the World War I days was still very much alive, more than twenty-five thousand men of the GWR having joined the forces during the conflict. Of these 2,436 were killed, and the bronze war memorial recording their memory still stands on Platform 1 at Paddington. Another feature of the magazine in the 1920s was the page entitled 'From People we have Pleased', passing on verbatim comments of customers and passengers praising the railway. Also included were numerous accounts of staff sporting fixtures which frequently spanned the employees of all the railway companies.

For all football devotees the highlight of the year is the Cup Final at Wembley, but it is perhaps not so frequently realised that the referee on the second occasion it was held there, in 1924, was an amateur, Captain W. E. Russell, who was a clerk in the GWR accounts section at Swindon.

Another feature of the magazine was its safety campaign, started in 1913. The safety record of any organisation is an amalgam of management initiatives and motivation, with attention to detail by those out on the job. There is no greater tribute to the successful *esprit de corps* of the GWR as a whole than its excellent safety record. When in January 1936 the collision at Shrivenham resulted in the death of a single passenger, it was only the second such fatality in 20 years.

This review has shown the Great Western Railway came into the grouping era as a large, technically advanced, closely-knit and safe organisation that gave employment for nearly one hundred thousand employees, and paid dividends of 7½ per cent for its thousands of shareholders, in addition to providing an efficient means of transport for passengers and freight throughout the area served by the eighty-eight-year old undertaking.

2

The Newcomers

The Railways Act of 1921 received the Royal Assent in August and was the first major legislative reorganisation that had been forced on the railways of this country since their infancy a century before. During World War I the need for greater coordination between more than 100 separate companies had necessitated a strong element of government control, and Winston Churchill in the post-war period had even proposed nationalisation. Ultimately the course adopted was to create by amalgamation four large new private companies, each of which primarily served a segment of Great Britain, although, as we shall see in Chapter 3, there was still considerable scope for competition along the boundaries of each company's territory. It was still felt necessary, however, to prevent the railways exploiting their near-monopoly of medium- and long-distance surface transport for passengers and goods. Accordingly, the 1921 Act also decreed that there would be an entirely new statutory system to control the rates and charges levied by the railways, and the resulting Railway Rates Tribunal was to exert its influence throughout the grouping era, and on into the days of nationalisation. At the same time, the Act set up the formal structure of Local Departmental and Sectional committees between the railway managements and unions that is still with us over sixty years later.

The separate railway companies, numbering over one hundred, as they existed throughout the country in 1921 were a disparate lot. The official monthly statistics published each month confined themselves to only about thirty companies, and even amongst these there was a very wide spectrum of activity. On the passenger side the monthly total of passengers carried varied between 23 million for the London Electric Railway and 117,000 for the Highland. Interestingly, the Great Western's gross receipts of £800,000 were easily the largest, and were more than double those of the underground lines in London. The 1921 Act thus had to recognise these differences and in the formation of the four new groups there were constituent and subsidiary companies, only the former having powers to appoint directors to the boards of the new organisation.

In view of the Great Western's predominant position in the country's railway system, coupled with its geographical coverage of the lines from London to Wales and the West of England, it had an unassailable right to form the nucleus of the new Western Group. Indeed, at one stage that company was arguing that it should be the *only* constituent company, with all the other railways merely being absorbed. However, the major Welsh lines raised considerable objection to this course of action, the Barry

Railway pointing out that their dividend of 10 per cent on the ordinary stock was higher than the Great Western's. As a result the six major Welsh lines were, together with the GWR, specified as constituents of the new Western Group, although each only nominated a single director to the enlarged Great Western board.

Although the 1921 Act made provision for each of the new corporate arrangements to be approved by the Railways Amalgamation Tribunal, there was no fixed date for the change-over to take place. In certain instances there were clearly advantages in getting on with the reorganisation, and not all the amalgamations took place on 1 January 1923. The London & North Western and Lancashire & Yorkshire Railways combined a year earlier, and the same date saw the amalgamation of all the constituent companies in the Western Group, together with the absorption of five of its subsidiary companies. Table 1 gives the names of the constituent railways and also provides a very brief comparison of their physical size and assets.

It is not possible within the scope of this book to do more than touch on the financial details of the amalgamations and absorptions. Indeed the 'Railway Returns' for 1921 ran to no less than 280 foolscap pages. (Those for 1922 were appreciably slimmer, and were prepared under one of the Assistant Secretaries at the Ministry of Transport, a Mr Cyril Hurcomb, who was, twenty-five years later, to become the first chairman of the nationalised British Transport Commission.) There is, however, one financial point that needs to be made to put the figures in my tables into perspective. The only figures I have quoted for the dividends are those on the *ordinary* stock, which is the usual yardstick by which the success of a company is judged. In making comparisons, however, it is necessary to take into account the financial 'gearing' of a company, or the ratio between the amount of

capital represented by the ordinary stock and that covered by all the fixed interest stock of various sorts which has a prior call on the profits of the company. Thus in the case of the Alexandra Docks & Railway its 5 per cent dividend on the ordinary stock represented only 28 per cent of its total interest payments, whereas the corresponding figure for the GWR was 48 per cent. Put another way, if the money available for distribution on the Alexandra Docks & Railway had fallen by 15 per cent, the dividend on the ordinary stock would have had to be halved. With the GWR the total distribution would have had to fall by nearly 25 per cent to affect the ordinary shareholders to the same extent.

The absorption of the various subsidiary companies was much more protracted, and is outlined in Table 2. Five companies were taken over at the beginning of 1922, with an additional eight in mid-year. January 1, 1923, saw the biggest single batch of ten being absorbed, although the incorporation of the Didcot Newbury & Southampton Railway was in fact officially back-dated by nearly two months in order to be included in this total. The three remaining companies involved in the 1921 Act were absorbed in mid-1923, but on the same date there was a further, quite separate, amalgamation. This was the take-over of the Swansea Harbour Trust, under separate legislation, the Great Western Railway (Swansea Harbour Vesting) Act of 1923, which will be discussed in Chapter 4.

Space does not permit a detailed account of all the companies that joined forces with the GWR to form the Western Group, but we ought to consider the six constituent companies because they formed a very significant addition to the Paddington empire. With the exception of the Cambrian, they were all built primarily to serve the collieries of South Wales, and hauled prodigious quantities of coal to the ports on the north coast of the Bristol Channel, for shipment or to bunker ships calling there. It will thus be appropriate to consider these first.

The geography of the South Wales coalfield dictated that the railways primarily followed the valleys stretching inland from the ports which were developed, frequently by the railway companies themselves, to provide the main outlets for their predominantly mineral traffic. The Great Western main line, however, crossed all their tracks along the relatively level coastal stretches, and so already provided an alternative railbourne route eastwards to the markets of England. The GWR had also developed its own extensive branch network into and across some of the valleys where the Welsh companies had not beaten them to it. The relatively narrow ridges between the Welsh valleys meant that it was at times possible for a railway to tunnel through into the next valley in order to provide a competitive outlet. Ferocious gradients were commonplace, with bridges across the rapidly-flowing watercourses whenever the valleys twisted too rapidly for the railway tracks to remain on the same side of the river. The civil engineering requirements often necessitated the construction of lofty structures, particularly on the cross-valley lines, the most striking being the Great Western's Crumlin Viaduct, striding across the valley with its lattice-girder spans perched on the similarly-constructed piers.

The largest and oldest of the South Wales companies was the Taff Vale, whose origin dated back to 1836, making it only a year younger than the Great Western itself. It also shared the same engineer, Isambard Kingdom Brunel, but this exponent of the broad gauge very firmly recommended the adoption of standard gauge for the Taff Vale. For all the 'Little Giant's' breadth of vision, he clearly never foresaw that the development of a national railway network would require the easy transfer of passengers and goods from one railway to another without the need for transhipment. In fairness to Brunel, however, it should be noted that transport capacity in the Taff valley consistently fell short of requirements during the nineteenth century. In the earliest years, the Glamorganshire Canal from Merthyr down to Abercynon was unable to carry all the traffic being offered and in 1802 it was supplemented by a tramroad. The original Act of Parliament had included permission for feeder tramways to be constructed from any works within four miles of the canal, but did not stipulate to which part of the canal they should connect. So when the dispute arose about the carrying capacity of the canal, it was realised that there was nothing to stop the factory owners building a parallel tramroad that eliminated the canal bottle-neck. Thus was born the Penydarren Tramway, over which Trevithick made his pioneering steam locomotive journey two years later, traces of which can still be seen today. The tramroad was crossed at Quaker's Yard by the Taff Vale Railway, carried on Brunel's elegant stone viaduct with its octagonal piers, but that in its turn needed enlarging not many years later to take two tracks instead of the original single one. At its most prosperous the Taff Vale paid a dividend of no less than 17½ per cent and moved twenty million tons of coal each year, approximately equal to the whole of the present-day Welsh coal production, some 60 per cent of which is hauled by British Rail. As we shall see later, the Taff Vale's inability to move enough coal resulted in the formation of the rival Barry Railway in 1884.

The Taff Vale's territory, up the valleys of the Taff and Rhondda, lay to the north of Cardiff, which, together with Penarth, was its principal outlet to the sea. The axis of the main valleys in this part of Wales lies roughly north-west/south-east, and between the Taff Vale's sphere of interest and the Great Western's own territory stretching inland from Newport there were three main competing lines. Two of these came down from the north, the most easterly being the London & North Western's branch to Nine Mile Point from their Heads of the Valleys line across from Abergavenny Junction. The second was the Brecon & Merthyr Tydfil Junction Railway, which got somewhat nearer to Newport, where it made an end-on junction with the Alexandra Docks & Railway Company, the smallest of the constituent companies. The third intermediate line was that of the Rhymney Railway, which served the valley of that name.

As will be seen from Table 1, the Taff Vale Railway had the largest locomotive stock of all the constituent companies. Some were from their own Cardiff West Yard Works, although the vast majority were built by private contractors to the railway's own designs. That works also dealt with locomotive overhauls, but was closed by the GWR in early 1926. Some of the

Taff Vale locomotives lasted until nationalisation, by which time they had been modified to take various Great Western standard features.

One of their Class O1 0–6–2Ts, built at West Yard in Cardiff during 1897, has had a very long career. Sold by the GWR in 1927, it was used on the Military Railway at Longmoor until 1945. In 1948 it got back into the coal-hauling business again, this time in Co Durham, being finally withdrawn in 1960 by the National Coal Board. They presented it to British Railways for preservation, and as the only Welsh locomotive in the National Collection it was stored in various places during the following two decades. Then in May 1983 I had the pleasure of welcoming it back into steam after restoration by the Caerphilly Railway Society, under the guidance of the Welsh Industrial & Maritime Museum.

This locomotive is a reminder that the Taff Vale Railway, like many of the other lines in South Wales, made considerable use of 0–6–2 tank locomotives, which were well suited for

Table 1 CONSTITUENT COMPANIES OF WESTERN GROUP
As at 31st December 1921 immediately prior to amalgamation

Company	Issued capital (£ million)	Net income for 1921 (£)	Annual dividends for 1921 on ordinary stock (per cent)	Route length[1] (miles)	Number of locomotives	Number of passenger carriages	Number of freight wagons[2]	Employees[3]
GREAT WESTERN RAILWAY	101.00	6 188 433	7¼	2 784¼[4]	3 148	5 581	88 755	91 985
Alexandra (Newport & South Wales) Docks & Railway	3.66	194 875	5	9¼	38	4	690	1 707
Barry Railway	4.82	359 137	10	47¼	148	178	2 136	4 206
Cambrian Railways	6.24	122 970	nil	244½	97	221	2 274	2 358
Cardiff Railway	5.95	193 973	1	11¾	36	8	43	2 702
Rhymney Railway	2.14	165 840	9	48¾	123	108	1 194	1 923
Taff Vale Railway	6.42	454 654	4	112¼	271	312	2 744	5 690

Notes: [1] Running lines owned
[2] Including service vehicles
[3] As on 31 March 1921
[4] Includes Port Talbot Railway & Docks
Sources: Ministry of Transport Railway Returns, *Railway Year Book*

32

work in the valleys. The absence of any carrying wheels at the front end enabled the more weight to be placed on the coupled axles. This was a vital feature since the maximum amount of adhesion was required for slogging uphill with empty wagons as well as on the descent with trains of loaded coal wagons bereft of any form of continuous brake. In both directions the speeds were low, so the absence of any guiding effect from a leading pony truck was not significant.

The Taff Vale Railway is also notable in history because of its legal battle following a strike in 1900, when they successfully sued the Amalgamated Society of Railway Servants for £23,000. This undoubtedly led to the Trades Unions aligning themselves with the socialist cause. Many of the Labour Party's attitudes to railways and mining this century can undoubtedly be traced to events in South Wales such as the 1900 Taff Vale Case, as it was known at the time.

Second in size after the Taff Vale came the Barry Railway, a relative late-comer to the South Wales scene, having been incorporated only in 1884. It owed its formation to the fact that the Taff Vale Railway and Cardiff Docks were unable to cope with all the coal being produced by the collieries in the area, and Barry Docks were developed to supplement the facilities available. To this destination a maximum of eleven million tons of coal flowed each year over seventy route miles stretching across Glamorgan. A triple-branched network ran from Bridgend in the west, via Trehafod to Bedwas in the east, while the railway also had running powers beyond these points for freight traffic, as well as into Cardiff for passengers. The Barry Railway, like others in South Wales, exploited its passenger potentials extensively, especially where they would not conflict with their freight traffic. An example of this was the opening of

their extension to Barry Island in time for the August Bank Holiday traffic in 1896. Eight years later they obtained an Act of Parliament to enable them to operate their own steamers in the Bristol Channel, but the various restrictions imposed prevented them from making any profits from the four paddle steamers the Barry subsequently operated until 1910.

The railway had its own maintenance works at Barry, and pursued a considerable degree of standardisation with its locomotives during its formative years. Indeed after 1905 only ten more locomotives were put into service, but World War I took its toll with delayed maintenance that lasted until after the grouping. After Swindon had assumed responsibility for the 148 locomotives involved in the 1922 amalgamation, about a third were stopped for immediate repairs after the visit of a GWR boiler inspector. Barry Docks have, over the last two decades, become known throughout the world because of Dai Woodham's scrapyard where the last relics of the British steam locomotive heritage have rusted in the sea air, awaiting rescue by some preservation society or the finality of cutting torches wielded by the scrapyard's staff.

The Rhymney Railway was, after the Barry, the next largest of the new constituents of the Great Western. Their access to the sea was at Cardiff, and their fifty-one route miles stretched northwards up the valley to Rhymney itself, from which there was a joint line to the London & North Western at Nantybwch. A second line climbed over the tops to Merthyr and another junction with the LNWR, which enjoyed reciprocal through running powers to Cardiff. The first part of the system to be opened (in 1858) was the northern portion of the main line, which connected with the Taff Vale at Walnut Tree Junction. From here the Rhymney had running powers into Cardiff, but in 1871 opened its own line right through, after spending no less than

LCGB – Ken Nunn Collection

11. A pre-Grouping scene on the Cambrian: Aberystwyth station on 5 June 1920. The 4–4–0 no 34 started out in life as one of the Metropolitan Railway's 4–4–0Ts, built for them by Beyer Peacock. The Cambrian purchased six of them second-hand, in 1905, and ten years later no 34 was converted by its original builders to a tender locomotive. Although the six Cambrian locomotives of this class were taken over by the GWR in 1922, all had been withdrawn by the June of the following year.

five years constructing its mile-long tunnel at Caerphilly.

Like the Barry, the Rhymney bought its locomotives from outside contractors, but undertook its own maintenance in its works at Cardiff Docks. At the turn of the century, the rapid build-up of the locomotive stock necessitated the provision of more extensive maintenance facilities, and these were opened at Caerphilly in 1901. They were well-equipped, and after the 1922 amalgamation were developed by the GWR to become their main works in South Wales, being provided with a new erecting shop, based on Swindon designs, which was opened in 1926. They were to play an important part in railway operations until the twilight of steam, being closed as such in 1963, but still extant.

The Alexandra (Newport & South Wales) Docks & Railway Company was unusual in that its two short sections of railway were separated by the lines of two other companies (the Rhymney and Brecon & Merthyr) over both of which they had running powers. Originally incorporated purely as a dock company at Newport in 1897, they absorbed the Pontypridd, Caerphilly & Newport Railway, the two sections of which had been opened throughout eleven years earlier. As that railway did not own any locomotives, its traffic was initially handled by locomotives from two separate foreign companies. The 1900s saw services being worked by the Great Western and Taff Vale Railways, as well as the owning company. There were other complications, and, even for the first six months of 1922, the trains off the Alexandra Docks line still did not run into the main station at Pontypridd. Their passenger service was clearly of relatively little importance, and through trains were withdrawn between Pontypridd and Newport by this route as early as 1956.

The locomotives of the Alexandra Docks & Railway Company were undoubtedly a mixed lot. One of those that passed into GWR ownership was originally a double-framed 0–6–0 and had been built for the Metropolitan Railway but very largely unused. It subsequently passed into the hands of the Sirhowy Railway which was later absorbed by the LNWR. They sold the locomotive to the Alexandra Docks as part of a job-lot of seven 0–6–0 tanks in 1880, but in 1921 the former Metropolitan locomotive was converted to a 0–6–2 by Hawthorn Leslie. In this form it passed into GWR hands, being numbered in the section allocated for 0–6–0 tanks because the list supplied to Swindon had not been updated. The GWR withdrew it in 1926 and after trying unsuccessfully to sell it cut it up two years later. Another batch of ten locomotives in A(N & SW) D & RC ownership at the beginning of 1922 was of Mersey Railway origin, having been bought by the Welsh company in 1903–05 following the electrification of the line out of Liverpool. So while the traffic operations in South Wales could be managed and integrated by those with local knowledge, the mechanical engineering department of the GWR at Swindon was faced with a disproportionate diversity by the locomotives of the Alexandra Docks & Railway Company.

The Cardiff Railway was the smallest of the constituent companies, and is perhaps most notable for the fact that its main line had only carried a single through train. Until just before the turn of the century, the company had been purely a dock undertaking – the Bute Docks. Frightened by the potential loss of traffic to other docks fed by their own railway systems, they changed their name and statutory authority to become the Cardiff Railway by an Act of 1897. It was twelve years later that their line from Heath Junction on the Rhymney was opened at great expense to a junction with the Taff Vale at Treforest. The Marquis of Bute rode on the footplate of a train of twelve wagons containing coal from his own collieries, but after this ceremonial run the Taff Vale closed the junction, on the grounds that it was supposed by the Act to connect with their freight lines rather than the passenger lines. Litigation continued as late as 1916 in the middle of World War I, but it was the steel shortage during the second world conflict that caused the demolition of the Cardiff Railway's long-disused four-span viaduct at Rhydyfelin. Such was the bitterness of commercial conflict involving docks, railways and collieries in South Wales during the period that saw Britain's coal production reach its zenith. Surprisingly, part of the Cardiff Railway is still in use for passenger traffic, with a DMU service running the seven miles from Bute Road Station in Cardiff to the present-day rail-head at Coryton.

The five constituent companies described so far were all enmeshed in the competitive business of the export of coal from the highly industrialised valleys of South Wales. By contrast the Cambrian Railways were a rural undertaking, stretching across central and northern Wales. Their system stretched from Talyllyn Junction, some three miles outside Brecon, in the south, to Whitchurch and Wrexham in the north. At Welshpool the Cambrian Coast line set off westwards, dividing, to this day, at Dovey Junction to continue northwards to Pwllheli and southwards to Aberystwyth. Included within their orbit were two narrow-gauge lines, the Vale of Rheidol and the Welshpool & Llanfair, the latter, however, being nominally a separate company that was directly absorbed by the GWR in January 1923. These lines totalled some 300 route miles and clearly made the Cambrian Railways the largest, from the point of view of route mileage, of all the Welsh constituent companies, but their locomotive stock of ninety-seven shows how much less intensive were their operations compared with those of the coal-hauling companies in the south.

The Cambrian routes were not easy ones to work, with such notable inclines as the Talerddig Bank. Three miles at 1 in 52/56 form the culmination of thirteen miles of climbing eastwards from Machynlleth on the River Dovey, and even force today's DMUs into bottom gear. In steam days locomotives were hard put to cope with such stretches, and the lightly-constructed bridges and track have always severely restricted the choice of motive power. Even the largest of the Cambrian's locomotives were light machines. In the main, 4–4–0s were used for the express passenger services, and 0–6–0 tender locomotives for freight. Some of the latter, duly rebuilt by the GWR with standard features, were to last until the 1950s, surviving the passenger locomotives by two decades or more, although it must be admitted that none of the 4–4–0s had been built any later than 1904, whereas the final batch of 0–6–0s had been taken into stock as late as 1919. The Cambrian did not construct its own locomotives, but its works at Oswestry undertook the overhauls, a practice that was to continue after the grouping. The Cambrian's lines were also subject to operational difficulties, being single track for most of the distance, and on the coastal stretches subject to damage from storms as well as cliff falls. They did not, however, have to suffer the extremes of colliery subsidence experienced in South Wales.

As already mentioned, it is not possible even to touch on all the Great Western's subsidiary companies. However, there are some interesting points that arise from consideration of the list in Table 2. The geographical distribution is remarkable, with no less than eighteen out of the twenty-six companies involved being situated in Wales or the Marches. Five of the remainder were in the west of England. Many branch lines throughout the Great Western system had been built by independent concerns, even if they had been operated from the outset by the GWR. Most of these had all been formally taken over prior to 1921, and it is interesting to speculate why this had not occurred with the remainder. In the case of the Welsh railways, although the Great Western had developed an extensive network of its own throughout the Principality, the fact that there were other locally-based competing companies in the field made absorption difficult or impossible. The lines in the west of England are less easy to explain, and their continued independence in 1921 might simply have been due to their distance from Paddington.

The two remaining companies on the list were the Didcot, Newbury & Southampton and the Midland & South Western Junction Railways. Both consisted of rural lines running north-west/south-east across southern England, with their southern portions continuing well out of the original Great Western territory to Andover and Winchester respectively. In the case of the second company, it might even be said to have had its northern beginning on the Midland, as its name implies, which was borne out by the fact that its trains commenced at the Midland rather than the Great Western station in Cheltenham. Under the new thinking, however, they clearly came within the orbit of the new Western Group, even if the original companies had previously shown no great enthusiasm in combining.

Looking at the figures in Table 2, one very interesting fact becomes apparent: the more profitable a company was, the earlier was its

Table 2 SUBSIDIARY COMPANIES OF WESTERN GROUP
Details as at 31st December 1921

Company	Issued capital (£ million)	Net income for 1921 (£)	Annual dividends for 1921 on Ordinary Shares (per cent)	Route length[2] (miles)	Number of locomotives taken over by GWR	Number of passenger carriages	Number of freight wagons[3]	Employees[4]
Absorbed as from 1 January 1922								
Cleobury, Mortimer & Ditton Priors Light Railway	0.11	3 026	2	12	2	4	23	n.a.
Penarth Harbour, Dock & Railway	1.03	50 446	5¼	9¼	—	—	—	n.a.
Port Talbot Railway & Docks	1.69	121 737	9	22	22	—	—	738
Princetown Railway	0.08	932	nil	10½	—	—	—	n.a.
Rhondda & Swansea Bay Railway	1.20	67 023	6	28¾	37	—	—	324
Absorbed as from 1 July 1922								
Brecon & Merthyr Tydfil Junction Railway	2.07	66 577	nil	59¾	47	90	640	842
Burry Port & Gwendreath Valley Railway	1.98	18 656	10	21¼	15	30	27	n.a.
Lampeter, Aberayron & New Quay Light Railway	0.09	444	nil	12	—	—	—	n.a.
Neath & Brecon Railway	1.67	43 159	nil	37	15	42	133	327
Ross & Monmouth Railway	0.21	8 162	1¾	12½	—	—	—	n.a.
Vale of Glamorgan Railway	0.66	27 440	4⁵/₃₂	20¾	—	—	—	n.a.
West Somerset Railway	0.18	6 533	2¾	14½	—	—	—	n.a.
Wrexham & Ellesmere Railway	0.29	11 280	3½	12¾	—	—	—	n.a.
Absorbed as from 1 January 1923								
Gwendraeth Valleys Railway	0.13	3 855 *loss*	nil	3	2	—	29	n.a.
Liskeard & Looe Railway	0.09	1 213	nil	9	—	—	—	n.a.
Llanelly & Mynydd Mawr Railway	0.10	16 842	nil	13	8	8	39	n.a.
Mawddwy Railway	0.01	388	4	6¾	—	—	—	n.a.
Penarth Extension Railway	0.02	694	3³/₁₀	1¼	—	—	—	n.a.
South Wales Mineral Railway	0.25	2 744	nil	13	5	—	—	n.a.
Teign Valley Railway	0.15	12 159	nil	7¾	—	—	—	n.a.
Van Railway	n.a.	n.a.	n.a.	6¾*	—	—	—	n.a.
Welshpool & Llanfair Light Railway	0.04	1 196	nil	9	2	—	—	n.a.
Didcot, Newbury & Southampton Railway[1]	1.31	15 674	nil	42¾	—	—	—	n.a.
Absorbed as from 1 July 1923								
Exeter Railway	0.38	4 247	nil	8¾	—	—	—	n.a.
Forest of Dean Central Railway	n.a.	n.a.	nil	5	—	—	—	n.a.
Midland & South Western Junction Railway	1.65	24 947	nil	60¾	29	58	379	700

Notes: [1] Absorption approved on 22 February 1923
[2] Running lines owned
[3] Including service vehicles
[4] As on 31 March 1921

Sources: Ministry of Transport Railway Returns, *Railway Year Book*

formal incorporation within the Western Group. Only two of the thirteen companies absorbed in 1923 were paying a dividend on their ordinary stock, whereas only four out of the nineteen taken over in the previous year were not doing this.

As anyone who has followed the fortunes of a present-day company take-over will know, the financial arrangements involved are often very complex. The railway company share market had been sufficiently complex to justify the production of an annual publication *Bradshaw's Railway Manual, Shareholders' Guide and Directory*, but its 1923 edition was to prove the last. The Railway Act of 1921 thus had its early casualties outside the railways themselves. As already mentioned, there was great diversity in the financial structures of the railways in the Western Group, which consequently resulted in complicated take-over arrangements. The Van Railway, which was worked by the Cambrian and was in the hands of a receiver, simply had its ordinary shares cancelled, while the assets of the Gwendraeth Valleys Railway were purchased entirely for £17,000 in cash. In the vast majority of cases, however, there was an exchange of shares. In the case of stock, such as debentures, etc., having prior claims on interest distributions, the agreements by and large ensured that investors continued to receive the same income each year as they had previously done, by exchanging suitable numbers of the appropriate type of Great Western stock. For those holding ordinary shares, the prior fortunes of their company were to determine what they got out of the amalgamation. Each of the deals was negotiated with the company concerned, and subject to approval by the Tribunal. The actual deals that resulted were extremely diverse, the Teign Valley shareholders, for instance, only

getting 5½ per cent of the number of GWR ordinary shares that they had had in their own company, whereas those holding similar stock in the Burry Port & Gwendreath received 143 per cent of their former holding. It takes only a quick glance at the profitabilities of the absorbed companies, however, to appreciate the reason for this. Rather interestingly the Barry opted for their ordinary shareholders getting a combination of 5 per cent preference and 5 per cent guaranteed stock in the new company, rather than ordinary stock. It will be appreciated that the new Great Western had to have its capital powers considerably increased to provide the necessary head-room for these additional issues, and Table 3 shows how their capital structure changed over the period of the grouping.

Table 3   GREAT WESTERN RAILWAY STOCK
On which Interest or Dividend was payable

	31 December 1921	31 December 1923
2½% Debenture	1 713 471	1 727 037
3½% Loans	—	47 300
4% Debenture	15 278 014	25 279 314
4¼% Debenture	1 009 494	1 009 494
4½% Debenture	4 629 317	4 629 317
5% Debenture	3 021 145	3 234 645
5% Rent charge	7 610 002	7 708 241
5% Consolidated guaranteed	17 946 891	23 816 537
5% Consolidated preference	11 936 348	29 427 984
Consolidated ordinary	37 082 220	42 929 732[1]
	100 226 902	139 809 601

Note: [1] Of this ordinary stock, £467,835 did not immediately rank for dividend because of certain transfer arrangements under the Railways Act 1921
Source: Ministry of Transport Railway Returns

3
The Rivals

Under grouping, each of the four new railway companies was allocated its own section of the country in which rival railway activities were at a minimum. Roughly-speaking, if one took the map of Great Britain, there were four separate areas bounded by lines radiating from London. In the north-east segment the LNER held sway, and moving clockwise round the capital we had the areas served by the Southern, Great Western, and London Midland & Scottish Railways. There were numerous places where penetrating lines ran into the neighbour's territories, but it was in the areas immediately adjoining the boundaries where competition between the companies was still fierce, except where the Thames Estuary physically separated the Southern and LNER. Rivalry was at a minimum between the diagonally-opposite pairs, in our case between the Great Western and London & North Eastern Railways, whereas the Great Western was in active commercial conflict with the Southern and the LMS. In the latter case both companies served the industrialised conurbations of Birmingham and Wolverhampton by their own routes, capable of providing services that were competitive from the point of view of speed, whereas the competition between the Great Western and Southern was predominantly over the holiday

traffic for Cornwall, Devon and Dorset. None of these conflicts was of course new, as the Southern merely replaced the London & South Western, while the LMS was the successor of the Midland and the London & North Western.

The competitive edge was sharpened, nevertheless, since the grouping removed a lot of the internal competition within the LMS's and SR's own areas, and this enabled these companies to concentrate their resources on the single external rival rather than dissipate them internally. That was the theory at any rate, although, for example, the problems of welding together the mechanical engineering departments within the LMS were very great. It was not until that company had persuaded W.A. Stanier to leave Swindon and become its CME in 1932 that the Churchward locomotive design principles were applied, and the products of Crewe started to equal and then out-perform those of the GWR. This was in spite of the exchanges that had taken place between the GWR and LNWR as far back as 1910. For the GWR, which remained virtually unaltered, there was a change in that it now had fewer rivals with which to contend. This was actually a minor factor, since most of the Southern and LMS constituents could never have competed with them anyway. There was not much traffic stealing that could go on, for instance, between the Caledonian and the GWR or between the latter and the South Eastern Railway.

There are four main ways in which rival transport organisations can compete: speed, comfort, frequency and price. It is important therefore to appreciate what flexibility of this sort the 'Big Four' railways had in the grouping period, before we can appreciate the ways in which they actually competed.

One of the most powerful factors in any commercial situation is pricing, but under the legislation of the inter-war years there was relatively little opportunity for the railways to manoeuvre in this field. For many years now we have been accustomed to British Rail fixing its rates by 'What the traffic will bear'. Anyone in a railway preservation society seeking to send a vehicle or locomotive over 'Big Brother's' tracks is liable to find that the rate quoted is just a few pounds cheaper than the cost by road. The sophistication of passenger costing in the 1970s was even been said to have earned Mrs Thatcher's admiration in spite of her general dislike of nationalised industries. Not only do we have the whole spectrum of railcards and different types of return fares, but there may even be a different price to travel from A to B rather than from B to A, while on those lines with faster HST services the cost per mile is higher than elsewhere. Back in 1922, however, the rates were fixed nationally in terms of so much per mile, the only variation being where certain outstanding engineering works existed, such as the Forth Bridge, which for fare purposes was reckoned as being six miles longer than it actually was. The mileage rates for passengers and freight were furthermore fixed by the statutory tribunal, and any upward changes had to be argued out with them at great length.

It was, however, possible for the railways, either individually or in conjunction, to cut rates, but, with less optional travel than there is now, the scope for increasing the overall revenue was limited. This ability was nevertheless used extensively whenever it was thought such a 'concession' might induce passengers to travel over one's own line, rather than that of a rival. There are two particular instances of this that I personally came across in the final days of the grouping period. Provided one bought the through ticket in advance, the main-line fares were the same from Oxford to Cambridge via London or via Bletchley. Clearly the GWR and LNER thought it was worth getting less per mile for the 121½-mile journey via Paddington and King's Cross than for the 77-mile direct route which was almost entirely over the LMS. It is fairly easy to appreciate the commercial arguments for this, and for the fact that the fares from Barnstaple to London were the same by the Great Western and Southern routes. What was not so obvious was that the rate between Barnstaple and Salisbury by the Southern was calculated via Taunton and Yeovil, a route unlikely to be taken by very many travellers in preference to all the advantages of using the through trains to Waterloo via Exeter. The most extreme example of this application of competitive fares by longer routes was between London and Swansea. For the vast majority of passengers, the only route they would ever know was the direct one from Paddington via the Severn Tunnel, but the LMS (and LNWR) would quote the same fare from Euston via Shrewsbury and the Central Wales line.

Railway rolling stock has always been built with a long life expectancy, and when the system was at its most extensive there was plenty of opportunity for carriages to be cascaded from more to less prestigious services as newer and better vehicles were introduced for the premier expresses. Large quantities of capital were locked up in such a system, and there was

M. W. Earley Collection, National Railway Museum, York

12. Rivalry between the SR and GWR in North Devon did not entirely eliminate co-operation. The photograph shows Bulldog 4–4–0 no 3348 'Launceston' on a through working over the Southern Railway from Barnstaple to Ilfracombe. On the steep incline from Braunton to Mortehoe the six-coach train is assisted in the rear by a Class M7 0–4–4 tank. 'Launceston' lost its nameplate in 1930 as part of a move to avoid passengers confusing the train's destination with the name of the locomotive.

thus limited scope for any quick or radical change in this particular competitive factor. The railways were at times able to make limited responses of this sort to provide some obvious improvement for the traveller, but overall it did not represent a major weapon in their competitive armoury. For similar reasons it was not easy to make a drastic change in the frequency of services. Running costs with steam were always relatively high compared with electricity, where it has always been advantageous to provide a very frequent service to help maximise the return on the fixed costs represented by the new motive power and all the electrification work. Steam locomotives could not be used as intensively as our multiple-units can today and, generally speaking, to put on 10 per cent more trains meant investing in 10 per cent more locomotives and rolling stock. It was thus rare to find competition being countered by any dramatic increase in the frequency of the service, unless it was accompanied by electrification, which was never undertaken by the GWR. Its only foray into this form of traction was the part ownership of the electric units for the Hammersmith & City Railway.

We are thus left with the overall speed of the trains to provide the main competitive thrust in the days of the steam railway. Speeding up a train requires the construction of no additional rolling stock, and may even in certain cases enable greater use to be made of a given set during the course of a day's operations. Higher power outputs by the locomotive will certainly be involved, and these may be available from existing designs. If they are not, the continuing process of building new and better locomotives for the top link services also results in the earlier designs being cascaded to provide more powerful motive power for the other services, within the limits set by route availability. It is for this reason that overall speeds were such a significant factor in the competitive standing of any railway in this country both before or after grouping.

Since our railway systems have developed with the majority of the main lines radiating from London, rivalry in the way of service and speed has always predominantly concerned those routes that run to and from the capital. In our study of the Great Western's rivals in the grouping era we must therefore start with these routes. The frontier between the GWR and the Southern could be positioned roughly mid-way between their West of England lines to Exeter, via Castle Cary and Salisbury respectively. Within the wider commuting area for London, the two lines only really conflicted with their services to Windsor. Throughout the day the LSWR had run a through service from Waterloo at hourly intervals, taking sixty to sixty-two minutes, and calling at all the outer suburban stations beyond Richmond. As the recent refurbishing by Madame Tussaud's has reminded us, the GWR's Windsor station was fully appointed to deal with Royal journeys, but for the ordinary traveller the line between there and Slough was treated as a separate branch. In spite of this there were good connections with fast main-line

trains, and the quickest overall journeys were just less than forty minutes. Clearly the complexities of the Southern's suburban network prevented any faster trains at commuting times, but the lack of a change would have at least partially compensated for the longer journey times in some travellers' minds.

Moving westwards, Reading was the location of a pair of branch lines, one each way across the frontier territory. The Southern had their own station, served previously by both the South Eastern and LSWR, but there was no way in which their services to London could compete with the Great Western's. Like the GWR's line south-westwards to Basingstoke, the Southern's entry to Reading from the east was to provide the opportunity for the development of through services during the grouping era. Although lines within the GWR camp served Andover and Salisbury, it was not until we reach its Castle Cary to Weymouth line via Yeovil that we find further direct competition for the London passengers. Weymouth was important for the GWR because it was the base of its only shipping services in the English Channel – those to the Channel Isles. These were in competition with the LSWR's from Southampton, and at the time of the grouping the winter services by the two rivals both involved night sailings to the islands and day journeys in the opposite direction. Although overall times were generally similar, with an evening departure from Waterloo at 9.30 p.m. compared with 9.15 from Paddington, the prospect of a 2 a.m. change on to the ship at Weymouth did not somehow have quite the appeal of the corresponding transfer at Southampton just before midnight. After the wartime slump, shipping traffic at Weymouth was, by 1920, up on pre-war days. As we have already seen in Chapter 1, the GWR's shipping fleet was not exactly in its first flush of youth at the time of grouping, and the subsequent improvements in the services will be dealt with later. While the LSWR did not use Weymouth as a port, they had access to the town by the connection at Dorchester, and could provide very competitive timings to the resort compared with the GWR. On the other hand, to Yeovil the Southern could not achieve anything like the speed the GWR could to Pen Mill, its best time to Yeovil Junction, let alone the Town, being nearly half-an-hour slower.

It was at Exeter that the two companies' main lines to the west actually met, and there was the unusual feature that trains bound for London by the rivals' routes would be facing in opposite directions in St David's station. East of this point, the gradients that had to be coped with undoubtedly favoured the GWR, and this was reflected in the best timings at the beginning of 1922. In both directions the GWR was achieving times of exactly three hours to Paddington, while the best the LSWR could offer was 3 hours 35 mins in the down direction.

In Devon and Cornwall the spheres of interest of the GWR and Southern actually crossed over, with the latter serving the north coast from Lynton to Padstow, while the GWR made its way along the banks of the Exe and Teign estuaries and threaded the sometimes wave-washed scenic coastal section through Dawlish. Barnstaple, the chief market town of North Devon, was served by both railways, the GWR using the now-closed branch from Taunton. It could still just better the LSWR's timings, even with its crack 11.00 from Waterloo which ran non-stop from Exeter St Davids to Barnstaple Junction.

After skirting the sparsely populated heights of central Dartmoor to the north and south respectively, the Southern and GWR converged again at Plymouth, where once more London-bound trains in North Road station would face in opposite directions. The Southern's route via Okehampton was appreciably longer than the Great Western's, and although the latter's trains had to cope with the Dainton gradients that were the legacy of Brunel's 'atmospheric caper', the Southern's had to contend with a climb to the 950-foot contour near Meldon. Coupled with the 'Cornish Riviera's' daily non-stop run from Paddington to Plymouth, these obstacles resulted in the GWR's best time to this city being nearly two hours better than the LSWR's in 1922, and there was never any real competition in overall speed between the two routes during the grouping era. Back in the 1900s the LSWR had worked the passengers to London off the trans-Atlantic liners calling at Plymouth, leaving the mails to the GWR to handle, but that was in the days of the 'Great Way Round'. During the grouping it was the GWR which put up some remarkable running with boat trains from Millbay to Paddington, and its finest rolling stock was to be built for such services in the 1930s.

It is not always realised that Plymouth used to have quite an extensive suburban rail service, and the GWR was very much in competition with the Southern in this field. The GWR undoubtedly had the edge over the Southern with the location of its Millbay terminus right in the commercial heart of the city, while its line from Devonport to St Budeaux ran closer than the Southern's to the biggest single centre of employment in Devon, the Royal Naval Dockyard. The Southern took over at grouping the Plymouth, Devonport & South Western Railway serving Calstock and the mining areas at the back of Kit Hill in Cornwall. Two decades after Beeching this line still provides a link to Plymouth from the area between Gunnislake and Bere Ferrers that is not adequately served by the road network, thanks to the drowned valleys of the Tamar and Tavy, which only the railways were bold enough to bridge. It was only when

13. A very early example of the use of the title 'British Railways' on the entrance to the railway stand at the British Empire Exhibition at Wembley in 1925. The GWR reproduction of the broad gauge 'North Star' is in the foreground. Beyond it are the LNER exhibits, a coach and 'Flying Scotsman'.

the Tamar Road Bridge was completed in recent years that Saltash lost its suburban services to and from Plymouth.

Turning now to the second of the Great Western's frontiers, this lay roughly-speaking between the GWR and LNWR main lines as far as Birmingham. In the Black Country the railway system became very complex indeed, but north of Wolverhampton the two companies could still compete for services to Shrewsbury and Chester, while these rivals' joint line north of the latter gave the GWR access to the Mersey via the Woodside terminus in Birkenhead. It was undoubtedly the Birmingham traffic that was the most important, however, as we are reminded still by the half-hourly interval InterCity service between Euston and New Street.

In 1922 both the LNWR and the GWR ran their best trains to Birmingham in the even two hours, and much publicity was made of these services. In 1924 the Great Western published one of its popular posters which showed a bowler-hatted passenger, pocket watch in his left hand, congratulating the driver with the words 'Splendid run! Thank you!'. The main message of the two-hour service was closely coupled with the words 'Shortest Route', inviting those not well versed in their railway geography to conclude that the GWR was able to beat its rival's time to Birmingham. As we have seen, both lines were able to schedule trains in the even two hours, but the advertising department at Paddington had nevertheless managed to provide an apparent advantage by capitalising on what actually amounted to the fact that its trains' average speed was slower!

The GWR two-hour trains to Birmingham were, however, actually faster than their rivals over the continuation to Wolverhampton, by an overall margin of something like ten minutes from London. The LNWR was at a geographical disadvantage to Shrewsbury, with its long cross-country line from Stafford to Wellington where its trains took the joint line over the final stretch into Shrewsbury. Its best train in January 1922 was the 10.45 a.m. from Euston to Aberystwyth, which took nearly 3½ hours whereas the best of the two-hour Birmingham expresses out of Paddington reached Shrewsbury in well under 3¼ hours. It must not be forgotten that the GWR's own tracks turned north at Wellington, wandering via Market Drayton to Nantwich and so into the very centre of LNWR operations at Crewe. The Manchester section of the 10.00 a.m. from Bournemouth Central used this route in 1922, while the Birkenhead portion followed separately from Wolverhampton. North of Shrewsbury, however, the more direct routes of the LNWR gave the LMS a significant advantage over the Great Western. Chester is on the Irish Mail route, and expresses via Crewe could beat the GWR's by up to three-quarters of an hour, while the margin between the rivals' services to the Mersey at Birkenhead and Liverpool was nearly an hour.

With the Cambrian becoming part of the GWR, the frontier with the LMS now extended westward across the northern part of Wales to Pwllheli, reached from Paddington via Shrewsbury and Machynlleth, and from Euston via Chester and Caernarvon, with a reversal at Afonwen. The 1922 train pattern was remarkably complex in this particular area, a January 1922 Bradshaw entry reading:

Through Carriages, London (Paddington) to Aberystwyth and Towyn; also Through Carriages, London (Euston) to Aberystwyth, and Birmingham (New Street) to Aberystwyth and Barmouth. Through Carriage, Manchester (London Road) and Liverpool (Lime Street) to Aberystwyth.

The LNWR was faster to Pwllheli than the combined Great Western and Cambrian Railways, but still took over 7½ hours.

We have so far been discussing the rivalry between the Great Western and its neighbours on lines out of London, but there was one area in which there was competition on a non-radial route. The Midland Railway's main line from Birmingham to Bristol and Bath handled the heavy traffic between the South-West and the Midlands. As mentioned in Chapter 1, the Great Western had completed its own Birmingham-Bristol route via Stratford-on-Avon in 1908, which, even if it used the same tracks between Cheltenham and Westerleigh, did not have the formidable operating obstacle of the Lickey Incline. Although both rival routes could work to capacity on summer Saturdays, the Great Western line never really displaced the earlier route from pride of place. In the course of the latter-day contraction of our railway system, it was the Great Western line that was to close between Stratford and Cheltenham, although at Gloucester and approaching Bristol today's

HSTs follow the course of the GWR's rather than the Midland's tracks.

It was from the southern end of this tentacle of the Midland that there was a cross-country route that provided significant competition for the Great Western. This was the Somerset & Dorset Joint, the main-line of which wrestled with the fierce gradients of the Mendips on its way from Bath via Templecombe to join the tracks of its other 999-year lessor, the LSWR, on the outskirts of Poole. The most notable train to use this line was the Manchester-Bournemouth express, which started as an LNWR-MR initiative before World War I to counter the Great Western's Bournemouth-Manchester service via Crewe, already mentioned. The title of 'Pines Express' was not to appear until the late 1920s and was indicative of the way in which the competition from this route was being increased.

The Great Western took over the Midland & South Western Junction Railway under the grouping, which, running south-westwards across southern England from Cheltenham might in theory have been considered as a rival to the Somerset & Dorset Joint. The axis of the M & SWJ was however slanted much too far towards the south-east, reaching the LSWR main line at Andover, facing east. It wandered through the rural landscape of the Cotswolds, the Marlborough Downs and Salisbury Plain, even managing to miss making a worthwhile connection with the GWR's main line at Swindon. The GWR thus much preferred to develop its through holiday services between the Midlands and the south coast via Oxford, Reading and Basingstoke which served many more centres of population and was double-track throughout. There was rather an interesting legacy of the M & SW Junction's origin in that, even after the grouping, trains over it used Landsdowne station at Cheltenham. This was the former Midland station, now called Chel-

tenham Spa, and was situated a full mile from the St James' terminus of the GWR.

It will be seen from the foregoing account that there was still considerable scope between the railways for competition for passenger traffic during the grouping, although they were still capable of joining forces with developments that were to their mutual advantage. The cooperation between the Great Western and Southern over the development of services to the south coast from the Midlands is one example, and the potentials of these particular flows were to be realised to the full during the later years of World War II with the build-up to the Second Front, followed by the support needed by the allied forces during their final victorious campaign in Europe. The ranks closed significantly in the 1930s, too, with the increasing threat of road transport, both public and private. The Great Western and Southern Railways combined forces in advertising campaigns, producing posters depicting West Country scenes, for instance, which carried the initials GWR and SR. There were also joint ventures that involved all four companies, one of the first being an elaborate stand at the Advertising Exhibition held at Olympia in 1927. The title British Railways had even appeared at Wembley in 1925 at the British Empire Exhibition, as shown in illustration no 13. The accounting role of that main joint venture, the Railway Clearing House, was immeasurably simplified by the grouping, although their active assistance was still necessary with every freight or passenger journey that covered the tracks of more than a single company. They also had an important function in the whole field of standardisation, both with technical features as well as commercial practices.

We have already discussed the competition the GWR experienced from the Southern with their services to the Channel Islands. The other Great Western shipping services were between south-west Wales and Ireland. Competition with alternative routes via Holyhead, Heysham and Stranraer, all now operated by the LMS, was not quite so intense, as they served very different areas on the far side of the Irish Sea. The setting up of the Irish Free State had given more weight to this division, and the importance of the mail service to and from Dublin declined for this reason. In addition, the coming of the telephone saw the decline of these services from their one-time premier position, which had been exemplified by the LNWR's development of water troughs to help speed the Trent Despatches to London. It should not be overlooked that a very high proportion of the railways' shipping interests was involved in freight and goods traffic rather than passengers, the importing of Irish cattle 'on the hoof' being a notable example.

It is nothing like so easy to review the effects of the grouping on the railway freight business as it is with passengers. Undoubtedly the formation of the four larger companies did away with considerable internal competition, and opened up the opportunity to optimise the routeing of traffic. When one is being paid only that share of the overall income that corresponds to the proportion of the total miles covered over one's own tracks, there is a great tendency to route wagons the long way round. From the GWR's point of view the changes of 1922–23 were of little effect in this particular connection, but the formation of the other three groups enabled them to rationalise their internal routeings in the way the Great Western was already doing. It also meant that traffic originating just over the boundary would be harder to come by in the future. As an example, freight for Exeter from Wokingham on the South Eastern would after grouping be routed for its whole journey over the Southern, rather than being handed over to the Great Western at Reading. It was, however, the rivalry of road transport during the grouping that was to provide the biggest threat to all the railways' freight services, as distinct from the heavy mineral traffic.

There were some small internal sources of potential competition after the grouping, as the light railways and some other minor lines were excluded from the Act. The Great Western had to contend with the Weston, Clevedon & Portishead, running down the coast of the Bristol Channel west of the Avon estuary, but with net receipts of only £1,485 in 1921 it could hardly be considered a serious rival. It finally faded out of the scene in the summer of 1940 after the Great Western had taken over the interests of the line's major creditor; it thus ultimately became entitled to the Light Railway's main assets, including its locomotives. The narrow-gauge lines were also in the main excluded from the grouping, although the Welshpool & Llanfair, and Vale of Rheidol, being respectively operated and owned by the Cambrian, were swept into the Western Group. While the Lynton & Barnstaple became part of the Southern Group, this was exceptional because of its sale to the LSWR in June 1922. None of the independent Welsh narrow-gauge lines, situated as they were in GWR territory, was involved at this time, although later the Great Western was to take over the Corris Railway.

Overall, therefore, there was much for the enlarged Great Western to do in the years immediately following 1921, both in welding its constituents into the new group, as well as presenting a competitive approach to those other organisations which were able to offer rival services, whether railborne or not.

4
'Twixt Rail and Sea

Railways, even in their infancy, were closely associated with docks and shipping. Many of the horse-worked waggonways of the eighteenth century terminated at staiths on the rivers or estuaries of the North-East. It was from these origins that the North Eastern Railway became the largest dock-operating company in the world at the time of the passing of the Railways Act of 1921. The amalgamations that swept the railways of South Wales, with their associated enterprises, into the new Western Group have already been described, but the result was that the enlarged GWR, in its turn, took over that pre-eminent position. On a gross revenue basis their dock operations were some 70 per cent larger than the NER's. The Great Western's ascendancy was further assured by its take-over of the Swansea Harbour Trust on 1 July 1923 under the provisions of the Great Western Railway (Swansea Harbour Vesting) Act of that year. With the new concern came fourteen locomotives, while, a year later still, there followed the take-over of Powlesland & Mason, a company providing various services for the Harbour Trust, which owned a further nine locomotives of its own.

Although the Great Western Docks extended from the Thames at Brentford to Newquay and Fowey in Cornwall, the sheer size and importance of their post-1923 ownership of the South Wales docks must claim our attention first. This system, spread along some fifty miles of the northern shore of the Bristol Channel from Newport to Swansea, was primarily built to provide an outlet for the collieries of the valleys winding up into the hills from the coastal plain. However, over the years they had also been developed into a major gateway for imports. Swansea, of course, had long received metalliferous ores from Cornwall and elsewhere for smelting, and the steadily-increasing scale of iron and steel manufacture in South Wales had similarly outstripped the supply of native ores. There were, nevertheless, further factors at work in these ports' favour, one being the fact that Welsh steam coal was the preferred fuel in the days when ships were coal-fired. Bunkering activities, as distinct from loading coal into the ships' holds, were still extremely important in the 1920s. Clearly, there were advantages for a ship-owner to be able to discharge his cargo and refuel in the course of a single call. The railways had, furthermore, invested heavily in what we would these days call the infrastructure of their Welsh ports. There was thus not only an adequate provision of suitable wharves, cranes and warehouses, but the periodic surveys of the vessels, called for by the maritime insurance regulations, could be met during the same call by the use of one of the numerous graving docks and similar facilities provided.

Back in the 1830s it was Bristol's geographical position facing the New World that provided much of the economic incentive for the construction of the Great Western Railway. The South Wales ports were similarly well-placed to benefit from such trade, but were also at no great disadvantage compared with other ports in the south of England as the terminal for shipping services to Africa, the Mediterranean and the Far East. Indeed, much of the shipping using the Bristol Channel was liner rather than tramp traffic, the term 'liner' implying regularity of sailing rather than passenger-carrying, although the latter traffic was also catered for. It is this sense of the word that carries through to today's Freightliner services on British Railways. Quite large ocean liners stopped at some of the South Wales ports, the Canadian Pacific's 'Montrose' of 16,402 tons gross visiting Cardiff in April and May 1929, for example, while in the previous July the 'George Washington' of the United States Lines, having a gross tonnage of 23,288, called in the Queen Alexandra Docks there, sailing again on the next tide. One also suspects that in the days before radio was compulsory and when radar was unknown, the Bristol Channel provided a ship with an easier and safer landfall than the approaches to the English Channel whose guardian reefs had proved disastrous to so many vessels feeling their way homeward through the fog. Barry Roads certainly provided an admirable area where ships could await the tide for docking or for free space alongside one of the busy wharves.

Geography also favoured the South Wales ports on the landward side as well, with all the manufacturing activities of the Midlands lying well within a 100-mile radius, while the large proportion of the British population that lived in the same area could obtain its imported foodstuffs by that route. In the 1920s there were, for example, extensive fish docks at Cardiff and Swansea, with trawler fleets based there, plus their associated ice plants. Live cattle were regularly received in ports such as Cardiff, which was equipped with the necessary lairs were they could be kept until sold for fattening or butchering. Slaughtering and cold-storage facilities were both provided at the port, in addition to loading arrangements to permit the animals to be sent away 'on the hoof' by rail. Fishguard also handled cattle from Ireland where lairages were also provided. There were other specialised importing facilities for grain, suction equipment probing into the holds of ships to unload them and discharge their cargo pneumatically into the tall silos on the dockside.

The coal industry of the 1920s required vast quantities of timber in the way of pit-props and similar material, and facilities were provided in the ports to deal with such imports. Enormous piles would at times build up on the stacking grounds in the docks in order to cushion the seasonal nature of supply caused by the winter freezing of the seaways to Canadian and Baltic ports. Swansea Docks were also notable in the 1920s because of the rise of the oil trade, which had become the second most important traffic after coal and coke. Crude oil was imported and a high proportion of the products was subsequently exported again after processing in the 'immense refining industry established by the Anglo-Persian Oil Company', as the *GWR Magazine* reported in 1929.

While the South Wales ports undoubtedly benefited from some geographic features, there was one that complicated their operation. Tidal flows are so concentrated by the funnel-shaped Bristol Channel that ultimately, at the spring tides, the Severn Bore crashes its way up river as far as Gloucester. Such violent surges, however,

14. A coal storage yard. Several hundred loaded wagons occupy the sidings on the left of the two central running lines, in marked contrast to the state of the empties' sidings on the right.

are well clear of the main port activities, but these facilities do have to cope with a very large tidal range. To overcome the problems associated with such a rise and fall, most of the port facilities in South Wales were constructed inside docks provided with locking facilities that kept the water level virtually constant the whole year round. Not only had it been necessary to construct larger and larger sea locks to handle the steadily-increasing size of ships and the growing business of the ports, but extensive pumping equipment was also necessary to maintain the water level in the docks, remaining at work virtually continuously. The waters of the Bristol Channel carry considerable quantities of silt, kept in suspension by the turbulence, but once pumped into the relative stillness of the docks this silt rapidly settles out. The dock operators thus had to provide extensive dredging equipment of various sorts to remove all the solid material they had pumped in with the water.

The locks and pumping engines were by no means the only mechanical equipment associated with docks as extensive as those in South Wales. Absolutely vital to the successful operation of any port is the loading and unloading machinery. Cranage in fact contributed 14 per cent more in the way of gross receipts in 1924 than did the harbour and dock dues. Large numbers of cranes were necessary to handle general cargoes, and in the 1920s the vast majority of these were powered hydraulically. Heavy duty electrical equipment was beginning to be constructed, and examples of electric cranes were being installed, but, with the establishment of the National Grid still nearly a decade off, the railways frequently had to construct their own electricity generating facilities for their docks. It is not often realised how extensive hydraulic power was the transmission before the electrical revolution. In large cities, such as London, high-pressure mains below the streets were used to provide power for lifts and other purposes such as the stage curtains in theatres. The Charing Cross Hotel in London, for instance, still used a hydraulic ram for its main visitor lift after World War II, and hydraulic capstans were widely used to move wagons within the confines of large railway goods depots. It was probably in the large docks, however, that the hydraulic power systems were seen at their most extensive. Not only were the lock gates moved by rams, but dozens of hydraulic cranes and hoists lined the sides of wharves, transferring loads between the ships and the lines of wagons being moved along with the aid of hydraulic capstans. Further extensions to the hydraulic systems were provided by the GWR in South Wales during the 1920s, although the hydraulic systems now began to be powered electrically rather than by steam. However, the greater operating flexibility of the electric level-luffing crane was starting to make it the preferred type of new equipment to be provided. Nevertheless, hydraulic cranes worked on in the South Wales Docks until after nationalisation in 1948.

By far the most extensive form of loading equipment in the South Wales ports was the coal hoist. The use of hopper wagons had not developed in the Welsh coalfield as it had done in the North-East, and this necessitated the tipping of every coal wagon to discharge its load of coal through an end door. As ships increased in size and freeboard, so it became necessary to lift each wagon higher in order to clear the hatch comings. This in turn increased the possibility of coal being broken as it fell into the depths of the hold, although the relatively hard steam coal from the Welsh valleys was fortunately less susceptible to such damage. The use of the Lewis-Hunter cranes that lifted boxes of coal into holds for discharge at a low level actually declined during the 1920s. The first experimental anti-breakage coal loading device was installed at Swansea during 1929 and their use later became widespread. Another complication that faced the railway docks in South Wales was the fact that much of the coal was for bunkering purposes. Instead of being loaded into the holds through relatively large horizontal openings, bunker fuel needed to be fed into much smaller openings, set high on the vessel to permit the coal to flow by gravity to the stokers in their boiler-rooms. In spite of all these difficulties, the rate at which coal could be loaded was amazing. Loading rates of more than 350 tons/hour could be maintained for long periods with a single hoist, and since this was with the average ten-ton coal wagon it represents the maintenance of a discharge rate of one wagon every minute-and-a-half.

One of the biggest developments of the mid-1920s in the South Wales railway coal trade was the introduction by the GWR of the twenty-ton steel wagon in 1924. Until then there were over 100,000 privately-owned ten-ton wooden wagons in circulation in the Welsh mining area, and the GWR saw the opportunity to bring about a radical improvement in the handling of coal by introducing a new design. On 10 September 1923, Felix Pole, the General Manager of the GWR, wrote to the South Wales coal traders proposing the introduction of the improved vehicles, and coal was tipped out of the first of them at Port Talbot Docks on 27 August the following year. By comparison with the time taken by British Railways, the National Coal Board and the CEGB to introduce 'Merry-go-Round' coal trains, such a rapid introduction seems unbelievable. It was undoubtedly facilitated by the railway's ownership of the docks and their willingness to modify their own discharging equipment. Rebates in haulage and tipping rates were offered to users of the new wagons and within a year eleven firms had already adopted them or had started to arrange for their use. Each of the new wagons cost only half as much to construct as a *pair* of wooden ten-tonners, and there was the additional advan-

15. Lady Pole, wife of Sir Felix, the General Manager of the GWR, opened the Palmer Swansea Dry Dock in June 1924. The first ship to enter was SS 'British Empress', suitably decked out in bunting for the occasion. A tug steadies her at the stern.

tage that a train of twenty-tonners was only just over 60 per cent of the length of one of wooden wagons carrying the same weight of coal. Another operating advantage was that the new wagons had doors at both ends, thus avoiding the need to turn the previous type of wagon from time to time. The use of the new wagons was extended to Cardiff, Swansea, Newport and Barry in 1925, and the Great Western had by that time committed some £2m for forty-nine new or modified tipping appliances to accommodate them, one half of which were in operation at the beginning of 1926. Collieries had also begun to acquire their own wagons to the new design.

One of the perennial problems that faces any dock organisation is the totally different scale of unit load by sea and land. A modest collier of the 1920s would take several thousand tons of coal, whereas the wagon load was only ten tons (or twenty in the case of the new wagons), and even a whole train represented a small proportion of the capacity of a sea-going vessel. The economics of successful shipping operations have always necessitated the quickest possible rates of loading and discharging in ports, and it was thus necessary to ensure the rapid availability of vast quantities of coal, ready for the arrival of the ship. With the collieries being mainly situated in the narrow valleys, there was little opportunity of being able to hold appreciable quantities of coal in their own sidings; in any case, the

52

maintenance of output (and hence the profitability of the pit) depended on the constant removal of the mined coal. The arrival of the expected ship could also be delayed by storms at sea, and as a result the railways had to provide vast siding storage capacity in the vicinity of the docks. Those inland of Newport Docks, for instance, were capable of holding no less than 12,000 wagons.

There was another complication the railways had to cope with, and this was caused by the merchandising arrangements for the coal. Right up to the time the ship docked, competitive offers could still be being made for the contract to provide that particular load, and each of the commercial contenders would need to have at least a starting quantity of his coal within easy access of the port. The South Wales Coal Marketing Scheme, designed to prevent unnecessary competition, was introduced at the end of the 1920s and must have also directly helped the railway's operations. Blending of different coals also took place, an operation facilitated by the provision of three or four 'loaded' sidings leading up to each hoist. Unlike the practice in the North-East, weighing took place as the wagons passed on and off the hoist, so there was no need for the time-consuming process of passing whole trains over the weighbridge at the colliery before despatch. It is not surprising therefore that sidings represented 60 per cent of the Barry Railway's tracks, while with the Alexandra (Newport & South Wales) Docks & Railway the figure was as high as 84 per cent, compared with only 24 per cent for the GWR.

During the 1920s various changes took place in the working practices at the docks. An attempt had been made to introduce a night shift of coal tippers and trimmers, but after an experimental period of six months in 1923, it was impossible to obtain agreement on the continuation of the practice. Following the General and Coal Strikes of 1926, however, two split shifts – day and night – with intervals between them, were adopted in February 1927. Another change took place in the loading of steel plate. The vast quantities of tinplate, galvanised steel, and the ordinary 'black' variety were normally handled in flat wooden boxes, and special equipment was provided to avoid damage being caused to them when they were being craned onto the ships. The practice of loading direct from wagon to ship had been on the increase, but the lower handling costs were more than counterbalanced by the slower loading rates and the consequent congestion caused. The GWR thus brought a new 'free alongside' arrangement into effect at Swansea by adjusting rates and stipulating that all the material was passed through the transit sheds. This is another example of the way in which the railway constantly optimised its dock operations.

We have so far concentrated our attention on the massive dock complexes in South Wales that the Great Western acquired under grouping, but we must also consider some of the other ports they owned either wholly or jointly. The full list is as follows:

Wholly owned		Jointly owned
Aberdovey	Llanelly	Chelsea
Barry	Newport	Fishguard
Brentford	Newquay	Lydney
Bridgwater	Penarth	Neyland
Briton Ferry	Plymouth	Rosslare
Burry Port	Port Talbot	
Cardiff	Saltney	
Fowey	Swansea	

A further thirty-nine ports were also served by the GWR. Space does not permit an account even of each of the wholly-owned docks, but mention must be made of some of them to

16. A demonstration of one of the new GWR twenty-ton coal wagons in August 1924. It is being compared with one of the seven-plank, twelve-ton variety which was larger than the average privately-owned type which carried only ten tons.

indicate the diversity of the Great Western's dock operations. None of the others had the magnitude of any of the South Wales group, but maritime trade in the 1920s was not all carried out in the large ocean-going vessels that frequented the Bristol Channel. When I was taken for my afternoon walks in the early 1930s, one of the favourite destinations was the City Basin at Exeter, now the location of an excellent maritime museum. Coal for the city's gas works arrived up the canal from Turf by coaster, and was grabbed out of the hold by a steam crane. As each rail wagon was filled, it was removed from the dock-side by the works' tank locomotive, resplendent with its brass-covered dome. This operation was typical of those going on all round the coastline of this country.

Observant travellers between Heathrow Airport and Central London by bus or train may note the single-track branch line crossing their route east of Osterley. This is what remains of the Great Western's Brentford branch from the main line at Southall, which no longer actually extends as far as the docks on the Thames. In the 1920s this was extremely active, with cargo being transferred between rail and barge, the latter acting as the link with ocean-going vessels using London Docks. Small sea-going vessels arrived direct from the Continent after Customs facilities had been negotiated, while the picturesque Medway sailing barges could also be seen. Extensive warehousing and siding facilities were also provided, and some of the hydraulic cranes were capable of making as many as sixty-nine lifts an hour. The year 1928 saw the building of a new shed at Brentford to handle the export of cars from 'Messrs. Morris Motors Ltd'. These came by train from Cowley already packed in cases and were transferred from rail to barge to travel down-river to the waiting ships in London Docks. This was the sole route for the export of Morris cars and was designed for an annual trade of 12,000 to 20,000 vehicles. In 1926 the export of a number of Metropolitan-

Cammell passenger rail carriages for Egypt took place via Brentford, while others were handled at Newport.

Much further west, the Great Western's docks at Millbay in Plymouth were very active, and were particularly noted for the connections they provided with trans-Atlantic liners. To an age which can reach New York by Concorde at the speed of a rifle bullet, enabling passengers to arrive earlier by the clock than they set off, it is hard to imagine the competition between the rival 'ocean greyhounds' during the first half of the twentieth century. Then as now, the business traveller wanted to reach his destination at the earliest possible moment, and there were thus advantages in a ship making a port of call at the first opportunity and transferring passengers to a specially-provided train. Before World War I, when Liverpool was the cradle of the trans-Atlantic business, calls were made at Fishguard to enable passengers to be whisked eastwards to London over the GWR. Plymouth had similarly become a port of call for Continental-bound liners, but after World War I it was British ships that started to put ashore some of their London-bound passengers at Plymouth before serving Cherbourg *en route* for Southampton. Cunard adopted this routine in September 1924 and gave the Great Western a wonderful opportunity to show what could be done in the way of fast running to London with their Ocean Liner specials. The dock at Plymouth was not large enough to permit the liners to enter the port itself, and the GWR used its own steam tenders to transfer passengers and mails between the liner in the Sound and their passenger terminal at Millbay. To load the mails on to the train at the dock, an electric belt conveyor was installed early in 1927, enabling the manpower requirements to be cut by two-thirds compared with the previous system using a human chain. A quarter of a century later I recall watching a similar chain transferring mail on to the Dun Laoghaire ferry at Holyhead. The number of calls by ocean liners at Plymouth more than doubled from 354 in 1921 to 788 in 1929, with the annual passenger total rising to over 38,000.

The naming in 1982 of a Class 37 diesel-electric locomotive 'William Cookworthy', after the pioneer of the Cornish china clay industry, is a reminder that even today this is an important source of business for British Railways. Won by hydraulic mining from the pits in the high ground to the north of St Austell and on the western fringes of Dartmoor, much of the clay has always been shipped overseas from the installations built by the Great Western Railway on the River Fowey. Although the estuary is little more than 100 yards wide in places up-river of the town itself, the drowned valley is deep enough for ocean-going ships, and a series of loading jetties were built along the right bank. They were served by rail from two directions. The single-track branch from Lostwithiel followed the river, in places cutting a corner so that it was lapped by water on both sides at high tide. From the other direction, the former Cornwall Minerals Railway was opened from Fowey to Newquay in 1874 and connected St Blazey, the railway's operating hub for the china clay traffic, through the 1,173-yard Pinnock Tunnel to join the other route at Fowey. Loaded trains had to slog up the 1 in 50 from behind the sand-dunes at Par to the tunnel entrance. A tight-fitting door was vital on the guard's van as the train traversed the murky depths of the longest tunnel in Cornwall before emerging carefully into the daylight again to enable most of the wagon's brakes to be pinned down for the even more precipitous descent at 1 in 40 to the Fowey Estuary. Although traversed briefly by diesel-hydraulics, the line has now been concreted over, and ECLP road vehicles trundle their way to the jetties through Pinnock Tunnel. The passenger service by this route was withdrawn as early as July 1929, 35½ years before the Beeching cuts saw the last of the auto-trains to Fowey from Lostwithiel.

Many visitors to Newquay today will turn down the pedestrian way that runs westwards along the cliff edge from the main road near the railway station. As they stroll through the cutting with its profusion of wild flowers, few will probably question the existence of an over-bridge part-way along, and only the most observant will spot the wire-fence supports made out of rusting bridge-rail. This was once the route of the Newquay Harbour Branch, only closed in 1926, which reached the quays by a rope-worked incline through a tunnel, the northern portal of which can still be identified in the cliff face behind the harbour. Further west, the small harbour at Portreath was similarly served by an incline at the end of the branch through Illogan that joined the main line west of Redruth, but that port itself was not owned by the railway. The Great Western had inherited this line from the West Cornwall Railway, but, although dating from the late 1830s, it was in fact the second line to serve that port. The first, opened in 1809, was the horse-worked Poldice Tramroad, the remains of which can still be traced running up the valley to the mines of the Scorrier and St Day area. Although the standard-gauge incline had superseded the earlier line, it too went out of use in 1936, there no longer being any worthwhile trade in ore from the mines to Swansea, matched, in the opposite direction, by the carrying of coal for the numerous mine engines of West Cornwall. Another of the Great Western's West Country shipping developments in 1925 was when they took over the direct operation of the Kingswear-Dartmouth ferries.

The Great Western Railway did much to exploit its dock business, a separate department being created, which at the beginning of 1927 also assumed control of the company's shipping interests, formerly managed by the Marine Department. The headquarters of the department were at Bute Docks in Cardiff, but an office was opened in Leadenhall Street in London in 1928 to provide the company with a presence in the mercantile centre of the country. Elaborate yearbooks were produced for the benefit of regular and potential port users, extending to over 300 pages by the 1930s. As early as 1927, however, the ports had been the subject of one of W. G. Chapman's books 'For Boys of All Ages', published by the GWR, the title of which has been 'lifted' for the present chapter. In it, an imaginary small boy is taken on a tour of some of the South Wales installations, the various technical and commercial developments all being carefully explained. Like the British Rail Property Board of today, the Dock Department was only too anxious to encourage the construction of suitable factories and other facilities on their dock estates. One of the most remarkable was the thirteen-acre building put up by the Government at Newport in World War I to recondition brass shell-cases unloaded direct from the steamers bringing them back from France. After its brief eighteen-month life, during which as many as 5,000 girls were employed, it was stripped of equipment and bought by the railway for letting. Swansea Docks was also the site of extensive patent fuel factories, while all the trades and professions associated with ships and sailors nestled in and around the dock areas. It must be remembered that in the 1920s it was customary to discharge the crew when a ship docked. Any subsequent moves inside the port were carried out by riggers, a new crew being taken on in due course for the outward voyage. With shipping services covering the whole world, it is not surprising that the ports of South Wales were to possess

Table 4 SHIPS ARRIVING AT SOUTH WALES PORTS

Year	Cardiff	Swansea	Newport	Barry	Port Talbot	Penarth	**South Wales**
1923	6373	5338	4217	3805	1494	2234	**23 461**
1924	6367	5425	4152	3367	1773	2218	**23 302**
1925	5664	5059	3896	2836	1616	2160	**21 231**
1926	4149	3652	2369	1729	793	1095	**13 787**
1927	5599	4922	4392	2980	1631	1857	**21 381**
1928	5039	4630	4247	3149	1542	1827	**20 432**
1929	5188	5333	4350	3172	1825	2146	**22 014**

Source: Great Western Docks, 1937 issue

cosmopolitan communities, typified by Tiger Bay.

In spite of all their efforts, the fortunes of the Great Western docks declined during the period under review in this book. Table 4 lists the number of vessels arriving in the six principal railway ports each year from 1923 to 1929. Particularly notable is the effect of the seven-month coal strike in 1926, which cut movements by a third, in spite of the quite considerable importation of coal that took place. It is significant that at Southampton corresponding figures from 1925 to 1926 showed a drop of 2 per cent only, while the Port of London *increased* its traffic by a similar margin. Overall, between 1923 and 1929 South Wales lost 6 per cent of its shipping movements while Southampton and London increased theirs by 21 and 31 per cent respectively. From the point of view of the cargo handled, the position was even worse, South Wales showing a loss of 14 per cent on its combined imports and exports, while the increase for London was no less than 40 per cent. As will be appreciated, these trends had a marked effect on the GWR's gross dock revenue, which fell from £3.34m in 1923 to £3.09m in 1929. As can be seen from Table 4, the shipping arrivals in 1929 showed an appreciable increase after dropping steadily since the grouping, but this recovery was to be cut short by

the Depression. That year thus represented a 'transient recovery in the South Wales docks' activities, and in Volume 2 of this work we shall see the consequences that followed as their decline continued into the 1930s. There is no doubt, however, that the Great Western's docks represented a considerable business activity in themselves, and made an appreciable direct contribution to the company's profitability, in addition to the revenue generated by railway haulage of the cargoes to and from the ports. The annual results for the docks as a whole are summed up in Table 5 for the period 1923–1929.

Table 5 GREAT WESTERN RAILWAY DOCKS: FINANCIAL RESULTS

Year	Receipts (£'000)	Expenditure (£'000)	Balance (£'000)
1923	3335	2444	891
1924	3241	2651	589
1925	2822	2428	395
1926	1927	2098	*171 loss*
1927★ old	2966	2303	663
revised	3243	2752	491
1928★	2923	2529	393
1929★	3086	2526	560

★ The basis for calculating railway statistics was altered in 1927, and both sets of figures are accordingly shown for that year
Source: LMS Handbook of Statistics 1930–1931

5
Developments of the 1920s

Having thus set the scene for the start of the grouping era, we must now follow the fortunes of the enlarged Great Western Railway through the difficult years of the 1920s. Rather than chronicle the events haphazardly as they occurred, the developments of the first seven years of the new regime will be described under a series of different headings, but it is first requisite to consider the general economic backdrop of the country for the period 1923–1929.

Britain, along with the other European countries, staggered out of World War I anxious to set about building 'a fit country for heroes to live in'. The strained British industrial backbone, however, had to compete with the rebuilt factories and mines of our European allies, while Germany, forced to make 'reparations' for the war, finished up by supplying the needs of many of our pre-war markets. The United States too, in the vigour of its industrial expansion, was also increasing its share of world trade, and was owed vast debts by Britain. Inflation during and after the war had reduced the value of the pound in November 1920 to 36 per cent of its mid-1914 value, but by the end of 1921 the retail price index had markedly decreased so that the pound's value had recovered to 50 per cent of its pre-war value. So for many the immediate economic goal was to see prices continue to fall back to the levels of 1914. Unemployment had,

however, rocketed to the 2½m mark in mid-1921. Protectionist moves were made to keep out competitive goods with tariffs, and generally the average Briton thought it was the foreigners, and the failure of successive British governments to deal with them properly, that prevented their own country returning to its pre-war prosperity. In spite of the high unemployment, workers were prepared to withdraw their labour. The locomotive men on the railways struck from 21–29 January in 1924, and no sooner was this settled than the dock workers throughout the country came out from 16–25 February.

Coal had been the driving power of British industrialisation, but the economic situation facing that industry had curbed capital investment, so that the vast majority of the pits were producing at a loss. After a Royal Commission's recommendation of nationalisation had been turned down by the Government, the mine owners took up another of their recommendations, that the mineworkers were being paid too much. As a result the miners struck in May with the slogan 'Not a minute on the day, not a penny off the pay', the Trades Union Congress turning this into the General Strike. Buses, trains and other essential services were operated by volunteers, and after nine days the TUC went to Downing Street to discuss ending the dispute.

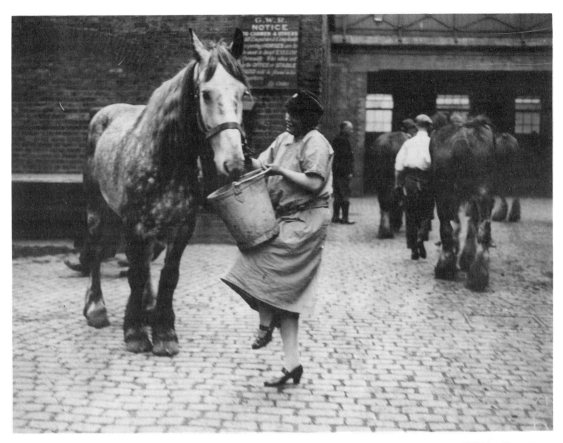

17. As well as giving male volunteers the chance to drive locomotives or operate signal boxes, the General Strike provided some opportunities for females. The Hon Mrs Beaumont was photographed watering a horse in the Great Western's stables at Paddington.

But, while the rest of the country staggered back to normality, the mines were to remain closed virtually until the end of that year. The loss of seven months' coal output was a severe blow to the railways generally, the Great Western, with its new-won empire in the coalfields of South Wales, being particularly badly hit. In the 1920s 'King Coal' was not a bad indicator of general industrial activity, and the figures in Table 6 show the quantities originated, not only on the Great Western, but nation-wide. By the end of the 1920s however, the coal industry had largely recovered, and the railway companies were benefiting from the increased business, while the total fall in freight tonnage was somewhat less than it was for coal. On the passenger side the situation was very similar, the Great Western's annual journey total falling by 9 per cent from 1923 to 1929, marginally less than the overall national decrease. As we will discover later, the passenger sector, in particular, saw great efforts with the promotion of new traffic (on a nationally-agreed basis), but even so there

Table 6 COAL CLASS TRAFFIC
ORIGINATED

	(millions of tons)	
Year	By GWR	Total for Gt Britain
1913	52	226
1923	50	222
1924	46	209
1925	41	194
1926	21	114
1927★ (old)	42	199
(revised)	43	196
1928★	41	187
1929★	46	207

★ The basis for calculating railway statistics was altered in
1927, and both sets of figures are shown for that year
Source: LMS *Handbook of Statistics* 1930–1931

was a 10 per cent fall in revenue over the country as a whole. With more efficient operations, all the railways achieved an increase in net receipts over the seven-year period before allowing for the 6 per cent fall in the cost of living that took place. The railways thus marginally improved their overall economic position in the years between grouping and the start of the 1930s, but only as a result of great efforts in every field of activity to increase their profitability.

Motive Power

When discussing the fortunes of any twentieth-century railway, the motive power must be the first aspect to consider, as it was the engineers' ability to provide the more powerful and faster designs that provided the competitive cutting edge which was to determine whether or not the owning company's fortunes prospered. It is a daunting task to provide the ability to generate some 2,000 horsepower within a cross-section nine feet wide by 13½ feet high (but with the

corners cut off), the whole having to remain balanced at speeds of up to 90 mph on twin strips of steel set only 56½ inches apart. The basic features of the steam locomotive had been incorporated into 'Rocket' by the Stephensons back in 1829, but a century later there was still the opportunity to fine-tune the design of steam locomotives to extract the last few hundred horsepower after coping with all the constraints that applied to this very specialised form of prime mover. Grouping had coincided with the appearance of the Castle class, Swindon's most powerful express locomotive to date, and they had managed to earn the Great Western a lot of publicity following the epic exchange trials of 1925 between them and the larger Gresley Pacifics. Four years later steam locomotive design on the Great Western was to reach its zenith with the construction of the Kings in 1927, and the railway, with its typical style, made the most of these impressive-looking and powerful machines, as will be described later.

Collett had taken over from Churchward as Chief Mechanical Engineer at the beginning of 1922, and 'Caerphilly Castle' appeared in August 1923. Externally the lines of the new locomotive were noticeably different from the previous four-cylinder Stars, with attractively curved outside steam pipes and a side-window cab which gave more protection to the crew as well as providing a better visual balance. The small 3,500 gallon tenders provided initially looked rather puny, but the use later of the higher-sided 4,000-gallon variety completed a well-proportioned design. The appearance of the class also marked the return of lining-out and the reappearance of the polished brass-work which had been painted over on the earlier locomotives since the days of World War I. Internally, the locomotives' main dimensions only represented a modest increase on those of the Stars, with 8 per cent more grate area and 12

18. The first of Collett's Castle class, no 4073 'Caerphilly Castle', attracts an audience at Paddington August 1923, its month of completion. The track layout and platform arrangements make an interesting contrast with the same station today.

per cent more heating surfaces, but the 14 per cent overall increase in nominal tractive effort was achieved at the expense of only 6 per cent more locomotive weight. These margins of improvement were just what the Great Western enginemen needed to cope with the increasing traffic, and the new locomotives quickly became established in the top links. The first batch of ten appeared in 1923–1924, to be followed by another ten new machines in 1925, and twenty in 1926–1927, in spite of the difficult economic times. The same period saw the rebuilding of some of the Stars to the new design, as well as the original Pacific 'Great Bear', which reappeared in its new guise as 'Viscount Churchill', named after the Chairman of the company.

The British Empire Exhibition at Wembley in 1924 provided a wonderful show-room for the newly-formed Big Four railway groups, and the visitor there found 'Caerphilly Castle' in close proximity to the LNER's 'Flying Scotsman'. In spite of the obviously smaller size of the Swindon design, a notice proclaimed it as the most

19. 'Pendennis Castle' steams out of King's Cross for Grantham on 22 April 1925 on one of the preliminary route-learning trips that preceded the actual Interchange Trials in 1925.

powerful express passenger locomotive in Great Britain. It was common at this time to equate power with the nominal tractive effort, and on that basis the GWR publicity people were justified. However, power is really a rate of doing work, not a measure of static pulling strength, and steam locomotives have to be moving at something approaching their normal operating speed before they can achieve their maximum power. Other things being equal, the sustained output achieved depends on the locomotive's ability to burn coal on the firebars. All was not equal, however, with Gresley's Pacifics in their early days, and this was proved dramatically in 1925 when, amidst great publicity, there was a full-scale exchange trial between the two classes. 'Pendennis Castle' operated between King's Cross and Doncaster, while the LNER Pacifics were entrusted with the 'Cornish Riviera

62

20. One of the Great Western Railway's exhibits at the centenary celebrations of the Stockton & Darlington Railway in July 1925. The Castle class 4–6–0 no 111 'Viscount Churchill' hauls an articulated train set past the Press stand at Goosepool. This locomotive had been rebuilt in the previous year from the pioneer British Pacific 'Great Bear'.

Limited' between Paddington and Plymouth, representatives of the 'home team' operating the same trains on alternate days. On both routes the Swindon design walked away with it, achieving better times and, more significantly, burning less coal. Even when 'Caldicot Castle' cut fifteen minutes off the timings of both the up and down 'Rivieras', her fuel consumption did not even approach that of the corresponding runs with the Pacific.

The LNER may not have been expecting the jubilation that broke out in the GWR camp as a result of these trials, but the sporting world has always loved to see an underdog win, and there had undoubtedly been some East Coast officials at King's Cross who did not even expect that a Castle could lift a sixteen-coach train up Holloway Bank. The LNER and Doncaster supporters have been crying 'foul' for one reason or another ever since, but Gresley altered the valve gear of one of his Pacifics in June 1925, and thereafter the full potential of the class could be realised. Not only was their haulage capacity improved, but fuel consumption dropped by a quarter. The first move had actually taken place

21. The Royal Visit to Swindon in May 1924. King George V
and Queen Mary inspect some of the moulders' art in the
foundry at the GWR Works.

in June 1925, a month before an LNER fitter
measured the valve vents of 'Windsor Castle',
up north for the cavalcade of that year, but the
final changes came in 1927. It would thus appear
that the cloak-and-dagger overnight work at
Darlington had provided some evidence of what
should be done, although, to be fair, the details
were already known. Once Gresley had decided
on the changes, Swindon's supremacy in the
British maximum power stakes was over for all
time. In 1926 'Launceston Castle', however, ran
on the LMS and her performance there showed
clearly the GWR's supremacy over the host
company's pre-grouping designs.

Back on the lines to the West of England and
Birmingham, the Great Western was beginning
to look for yet faster overall speeds, and it was
equally obvious that loads were similarly on the
increase. The construction of the Southern's
Lord Nelsons in 1926 had pipped the Great
Western with a higher tractive effort, which on
its own criterion meant higher power. The
GWR Civil Engineer could cope with an un-
precedented axle load of 22½ tons on the most
important routes, and so Collett was able to
extend the basic Star design to the limit. Compared with the Castles, the grate area of the
Kings was 17 per cent greater, the heating
surfaces 7 per cent more, while the locomotive
nominally weighed in at 89 tons, nine more than

64

22. All ready to depart for Baltimore, 'King George V'
works a train out of Paddington in 1927, complete with the
Westinghouse brake pump on the side of the smokebox.

a Castle. As a result the nominal tractive effort was squeezed up to no less than 40,300 lb and Swindon once again had the 'most powerful locomotive' in the country. The only unusual feature was the cranked bogie frame, necessary to stop it fouling the cylinders, and the resulting outside springs and brass-capped axlebox on the leading axlebox were always to provide a distinctive feature to a most impressive design. The first of the class was named after King George V, who had made an extensive tour of the Swindon Works in 1924 together with Queen Mary, the two of them subsequently returning to Swindon station in the cab of 'Windsor Castle'. In a blaze of publicity the first of the Kings was sent to the United States in 1927 to take part in the Fair of the Iron Horse, held to mark the centenary of the Baltimore & Ohio Railroad. The locomotive was given the honour of leading the daily procession as the representative of the country that had originated the steam locomotive. Having personally taken a British locomotive to an American railfair, I can vouch for the great interest generated, even if the replica of 'Rocket' did not quite have the majesty of 'King George V', and did not benefit from the equivalent of Miss Schueler who stood as Britannia in regal dignity beside the smokebox, equipped with helmet, shield and trident. The Great Western 4–6–0 ran some trials on the B & O during its visit, and still to this day carries the bell, presented by the American railroad, on its front buffer-beam. Its clean lines undoubtedly had an effect on American designers too, while from a general publicity point of view the visit was a *tour de force* for the GWR.

Swindon's activities with new locomotives were not confined solely to express passenger designs, as 1924 saw the rebuilding of 'Saint Martin' as the first of the mixed-traffic Hall class. It was not until 1928 that production of new locomotives of the class actually started,

and the basic concept was to be picked up in 1934 by Stanier on the LMS with the 'Black Fives', and later still by Thompson with his B1s for the LNER. Further still down the scale, the takeover of the Welsh coal railways, with their plethora of 0–6–2 tanks, prompted the Great Western to produce its own design with the same wheel arrangement in 1924. Successive batches of fifty were built over two-year periods from 1924 onwards, and by 1928 Swindon was not able to turn them out fast enough, so a final fifty were ordered from Armstrong Whitworth, but because of the depression many of the class were put into store on delivery.

As already remarked, the Great Western inherited a considerable assortment of locomotives under the grouping, and the diversity of designs involved clearly caused consternation to a motive power department that had been pursuing a policy of standardisation for two decades. Many of the Welsh locomotives could quietly be scrapped, but, with economy the watchword throughout the 1920s, there was still a place for those capable of being kept at work economically. Since boilers always had a shorter life than the frames, motion and running gear, the opportunities arose to substitute standard Swindon boilers as the existing pre-grouping ones became due for expensive overhaul. With the new boilers went the appropriate standard fitments, including chimney, safety-valve bonnet and cab. As a consequence, many of the constituent and subsidiary companies' locomotives quickly assumed some of the highly-distinctive Swindon characteristics. As early as 1925, one of the Midland & South Western Junction 4–4–0s had been so converted, and various tank classes were similarly treated, although there was at times difficulty in accommodating the new boiler between the existing side tanks.

The Great Western was notable for the use of

23. On exhibition at the Fair of the Iron Horse in Baltimore, 'King George V' stands in front of the Canadian National Railway 4–8–4 no 6100.

British Rail Western Region

pannier tanks on its shunting locomotives, the first of which dated back to 1898. Many of these earlier locomotives had partially open cabs, and in 1923 work was started to extend them over the bunkers to meet a new back weatherboard. The new 57xx class of locomotives of this type was ultimately to total no less than 863, construction starting in 1929 with an order for fifty placed with the North British Locomotive Company. The same period saw the construction of some more 2–6–2 tanks for suburban services, the basic design again going back a quarter of a century, although a number of more-recent design details were incorporated. Amongst other activities at Swindon, building of the smaller-wheeled branch-line locomotives with the same wheel arrangement had resumed somewhat earlier, in 1924, with a batch of twenty, and in 1927–1929 a further hundred were constructed with larger side tanks. This

H. C. Casserley

24. 0–6–2T – Swindon version. One of the GWR 0–6–2 tanks, primarily built for service in South Wales during the 1920s based on the existing standard designs. No 6606 was photographed at Swindon in September 1927 within a month of its completion.

25. 0–6–2T – Absorbed and modified. One of the Taff Vale A Class 0–6–2 tanks as fitted with standard GWR boiler and other details after the Grouping. This was TVR no 156, built in 1919 by Nasmyth, Wilson and was not withdrawn until 1956, well after nationalisation.

H. C. Casserley

spate of building that started at the end of 1920s was clearly in response to the rising annual locomotive mileage then taking place, which reached a record 97 million miles in 1929, with everyone hoping that the economic difficulties of the mid-1920s were now behind them.

Carriages and Wagons

As was the case with motive power, the immediate post-grouping years saw considerable changes in the design of new carriage stock, while, to match the readoption of the full splendour of the lined Brunswick green livery for the GWR passenger locomotives, the decision was made in 1923 to revert to chocolate and cream for coaching stock. These colours are so closely associated with the GWR that the possibilities of their use on modern stock in connection with the 150th anniversary celebrations was one of the points that was raised in the first of the meetings held in the Board Room at Paddington to plan the events for 1985.

Although there were to be a number of new technical features adopted on Great Western carriage stock during the grouping period, the basic method of construction did not change from what had been adopted before World War I. Steel panelling covered wooden bodywork mounted on steel underframes, and, although various small improvements were made at Swindon to enable the output to be steadily increased over the years, there was no dramatic replanning of the works in the interests of mass-production. There was, however, a notable improvement in style, at least to mid-twentieth century eyes, which started in 1923 with the adoption of a much cleaner external appearance. Smooth steel sheets took over from the fussy panelling, and the toplights disappeared, with, from 1929, the glass of the

26. The interior of one of the Great Western third-class sleeping cars of 1928. In contrast to the contemporary publicity photograph which showed four young ladies apparently fast asleep, one of the male travellers in this compartment appears to have been somewhat surprised by the arrival of the photographer.

BBC Hulton Picture Library

windows being far less deeply recessed than had been the case hitherto. Indeed the 1923 designs marked, from the point of view of the general appearance of their bodywork, the beginning of the style we know today. A simplified paint scheme followed the panelling changes, with horizontal lining taking the place of the complications of the pre-grouping days.

27. One of the GWR 70-foot third-class corridor coaches of 1925. The complicated lining can be seen, together with the garter round the 'coat of arms' and the separate crests on either side.

28. One of the bow-ended composite coaches built for the 'Cornish Riviera' in 1929. The lapse of 4 years since the previous illustration had produced marked changes in design and livery.

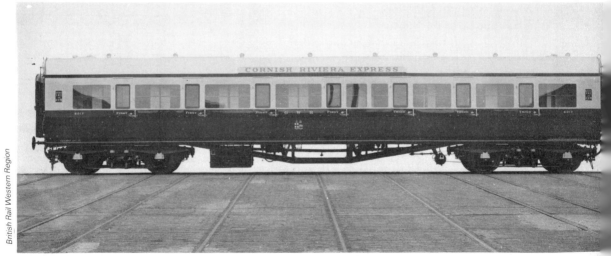

By the 1900s the GWR had adopted the use of 70-footers for the principal expresses, in the interest of reducing the coach/passenger weight ratio, but had found that there was rather more flange wear on the bogies of these vehicles. As a result, their construction gave way in the 1920s to the standard 57-foot stock. From 1929 a length of sixty feet was adopted with the windows nearly flush, while the sides were bowed to obtain maximum use of the loading gauge at seat level. Smaller bogies with a seven-foot wheelbase were used for some time from 1925 onwards, although the heavier nine-foot type were still supplied on the prestige stock, such as the sets built for the 'Cornish Riviera'. Coincident with the use of the smaller bogies, the coaches became bow-ended, this second feature being combined with the use of a new design of suspended gangway. At the time of the grouping the Great Western also tried out the use of Buckeye automatic couplers of the knuckle type, together with the Pullman gangway. It was the vehicles with this particular feature that first had the bow ends, but, with a relatively small number of set trains so equipped, there could potentially be difficulties with strengthening them at peak periods. One of the first seven-coach South Wales sets of this type thus consisted of two flat-ended brake thirds with ordinary couplers, three vehicles with double bowed ends and Buckeyes, and two that had the new design at one end and the old at the other. Other variants appeared later, but the special

H. C. Casserley

29. Motorail – 1920s style. Cars from Severn Tunnel Junction to Pilning just after leaving the eastern end of the Severn Tunnel. Although taken as late as 1958, the photograph gives a good idea of the accompanying passengers' view of their cars on this service which was introduced in 1924.

types of gangways and the Buckeyes were to disappear, the latter only lasting about a decade on the GWR.

It is Gresley on the LNER who is generally associated with the use of articulation for passenger stock, but the GWR invested quite heavily in it in the 1920s. Six express train sets of eight cars were built, but these were split into articulated units of 2 and 3 vehicles, thus minimising the potential difficulties that were to have their effect on the APT development fifty-five years later. One of these new sets took part in the Cavalcade in July 1925 that marked the centenary of 'Locomotion's' inaugural journey from Shildon to the River Tees along the route of George Stephenson's Stockton & Darlington Railway. This particular set later went into service on the Plymouth Ocean Liner specials. The articulation was abandoned in the mid-1930s, and the vehicles rebuilt with pairs of bogies. Some similarly-equipped suburban sets were also constructed for use on through services to Moorgate by the 'Widened Lines', and although these services disappeared for good at the beginning of World War II, all these particular articulated sets continued in use elsewhere until the late 1950s. So ended the Great Western's experiments with Buckeyes and articulation.

While at the time of the grouping the GWR decided to cut down the length of its passenger vehicles, it was at the end of the 1920s that they again started to make maximum use of the legacy of Brunel's loading-gauge. In July 1929, when the 'Cornish Riviera' began running to Plymouth with a new non-stop record timing of four hours, the King left Paddington at the head of thirteen-coach trains of new stock built to a width of 9ft 5¾ins. These included the first slip coaches to be built since the grouping, the use of these vehicles forming a significant feature of Great Western operations. A year earlier had seen the introduction of the first third-class sleepers. Until then sleeping cars had been provided for first-class passengers only, but the changing travel patterns of the 1920s resulted in the GWR, the LMS and the LNER agreeing to adopt common standards of accommodation for the new services. Initially the Great Western built three such vehicles, each of which had only three sleeping compartments amongst the eight compartments provided. Like similar vehicles elsewhere, the top berths could be folded away for day use. It is interesting to read the contemporary account of their introduction in the *Great Western Railway Magazine* for October 1928, which started

> During recent years many innovations have been made for increasing the comforts of railway travel, but it is doubtful if any has attracted greater attention than the introduction of sleeping cars for third class passengers. When the decision to provide this facility was announced a few months ago, it was acclaimed by all sections of the Press as further evidence of the desire of the railways to meet the wishes of their passengers . . .

The text was illustrated by a photograph of one of the new compartments occupied by four young ladies with bobbed heads, all appearing to be fast asleep in spite of the activities of the photographer with his lights. Not many of the Great Western's routes were long enough to justify the provision of sleeping car services, but the standardisation of the new facilities by the three separate railways concerned provides an example of the way in which the competing companies could nevertheless cooperate in matters of common interest.

By and large the Great Western built its own coaching stock, and Swindon increased its annual production of new vehicles from 210 in 1924 to 295 three years later. Well over 4,000 vehicles a year were overhauled, while on the freight side over 2,000 new wagons were constructed each year, with repairs exceeding the 15,000 mark in a twelve-month. The vast majority of the freight vehicles was devoid of any form of vacuum braking equipment, even a through train pipe, although fitted freights were beginning to provide an important marketing tool, as will be seen later. Types of railway wagons had long been identified by telegraphic names, but the Great Western tended to use these fairly widely, so that names like 'Macaws' and 'Siphons' became quite well known. The works was also involved in the construction of the railway's road cartage vehicles, 1928, for example, seeing the completion of 172 bodies for motor vehicles and horseboxes, while 196 containers were also turned out. Another item of interest dating from 1924 was the equipping of carriage trucks to take cars through the Severn Tunnel from Pilning (High Level) to Severn Tunnel Junction, a service that was to continue until the opening of the Severn Bridge. In 1946 the cost of taking an eight horsepower car over this route was only 6s 2d (31p), less than three times the ordinary third-class fare of 2s 4d (12p). So, if we should ever see the Channel Tunnel built, there is a British precedent for the conveyance of cars through an underwater tunnel of at least sixty years standing. The year 1927 saw the construction of the first twelve milk tank wagons, the glass-lined containers being owned by the United Dairies, while the underframes and running gear were built by the railway. Thereafter vehicles of this sort were a common sight, even on passenger trains, while there were overnight services to London just for milk from concentration centres such as Totnes and Lostwithiel.

The 1920s thus saw considerable changes in the carriage and wagon fleet, and with a start made on the standardisation of new coach designs, the 1930s were to see these reach the height of attainment with the construction of the Great Western's 'Super Saloons'.

Civil Engineering

Throughout the 1920s the Civil Engineering Department of the Great Western was spending just over an eighth of the company's total railway receipts each year on the 'Maintenance and Renewal of Way and Works'. The sums involved, 1926 apart, ranged between £4.0m and £4.6m, and in a normal year could equal up to three-quarters of the whole net revenue of the company. In 1926, thanks to the industrial disputes throughout the country, the Civic Engineer's expenditure was actually higher than the net revenue. To these figures must be added the civil engineering content of the £7m or so of new capital spent by the GWR in the period 1923–29. The size of the engineering organisation necessary to achieve this sort of performance, and the scale of its operations, is obvious, but one or two significant figures may help the reader compensate for the effect of sixty years of inflation. In 1929, for instance, some 500 miles of track were relaid or resleepered, using 37,000 tons of new rails and three-quarters of a million sleepers. (BR only renewed a total of 415 miles in 1982.) Work was carried out on eighty-five bridges, while the painting of buildings and structures required 370 tons of paint and 33,000 gallons of tar. The relative lack of power equipment with which to do the work must also be remembered. A publicity photograph, showing some of the sixty-four miles of steel-sleepered track being installed, depicted a gang of about twenty men lifting a rail-length into place *by hand*.

While the routine renewal of track and similar maintenance items is common-place in any railway operation, the years under discussion saw a number of major renewals of structures that dated back to the days of Brunel. While we have already remarked on the way some of his bridges are still in daily use sixty years after the grouping, there were many that for one reason or another had reached the end of their life in the 1920s. Notable amongst these works was the start made to replace the eight of his famous timber viaducts situated on the Falmouth Branch. This was a protractd business, with some of the timbers in the old structures having to be replaced in the meantime. Other wooden viaducts were reconstructed near Langport West, and at Hoodown on the Kingswear branch. It was not only Brunel's wooden viaducts that needed attention, his bowstring arch spanning the Usk at Newport being re-newed in 1924 as part of the widening and general improvements then taking place.

Another major event of the late 1920s was the replacement of the land-spans of the Royal Albert Bridge at Saltash, which had reached out towards the centre of the river some five years before the whole structure was opened in 1859. The original beams, with their rounded tops, were replaced with the deeper-section, flat-topped girders familiar today. An ingenious technique was employed for this work, with an 'erection-wagon' being positioned so that its ends were over adjacent piers. This then became the bridge, supporting the track underneath it while the old beams were lifted up by winches mounted on the wagon's cross-beams. These girders could then be moved outwards, enabling the new ones, already slung from the wagon's cross-beams, to be placed in their proper positions. After the support of the track had been transferred to the new girders, the erection-wagon was moved slowly back with the old beams suspended outside the bridge structure.

30. Some of the Cornish viaducts on the main line required strengthening in the 1920s. A pair of steam cranes are engaged on the task of replacing the spans of Liskeard Viaduct in April 1926, with a 2–6–2T at the lead of the engineers' train. In the distance below the left-hand crane can be seen vehicles in Liskeard goods yard. The line to Coombe Junction runs along the far side of the valley, between the white level-crossing gates seen under the right-hand cranes, before swinging back to run under the viaduct just off the picture to the right.

The engineers had absolute possession on Sundays for each operation, in theory from 9 a.m. to 2 p.m., although my father, who was living in Saltash at the time, used to tell the story that, on the first week-end, the occupation over-ran very considerably, with the first up and down trains being held for hours waiting to get across. On the other hand, after the engineers had got their

31. Reconstruction of Newton Abbot station which was
completed in 1927. The temporary arrangements seem
rather rough and ready with a few wagon sheets protecting
the bookstall. The prominent poster advertises the
Terminus Hotel at Bristol.

hands in, the work went very well, and on the
occasion when the Directors came down in their
special train to see one of the last Sundays'
operations they nearly missed it completely.

The lofty Crumlin viaduct in South Wales
was another major structure that needed frequent attention during the period, the girders
being strengthened in 1924 and then completely
refloored over its whole 1,500ft length, starting

three years later. Another Brunel structure, the
colonnade viaduct at Dawlish, was replaced in
1928, and the sea wall hereabouts needed strengthening in 1924 and 1927. The former seems to
have been a bad year generally with the effects of
the sea, work also being necessary near Afon
Wen and Llanelly. While not all bridge renewals
were quite so spectacular, or costly, as those
so far mentioned, there was a lot of important
work going on with smaller structures to enable
them to take the heavier locomotives, such as the
Kings. With the general increase in road traffic,
many bridges had to be widened, or totally new

75

ones were built at the request, and presumably at the expense, of the local authorities.

Throughout the period there was much station rebuilding taking place, with large schemes at all three major South Wales cities. The Cardiff (Queen Street) improvements provided direct junctions between the Rhymney and Taff Vale lines, and other new connections were made elsewhere in South Wales between the former constituent and subsidiary companies' lines. Newton Abbot was also completely rebuilt in 1927, the local population being so pleased with the result that they presented the public clocks for the new facility, which, together with all the others at the station, were controlled by a master regulating system. As part of the general celebrations, the broad-gauge locomotive 'Tiny' was put on display on one of the platforms, where it remained until I personally supervised its removal to Buckfastleigh over fifty years later. Station improvements were by no means confined to those handling passengers. Notable amongst the rebuilding of goods stations were those at Bristol and Paddington, both of which were completed in 1929. The former included an 'inground' warehouse in the reinforced concrete vaults below the tracks. No less than 408 wagons could be handled under cover at one time. East Depot at Bristol was the location of a new hump yard, opened in 1923.

No department on the GWR in the 1920s needed much exhortation to seek financial economies, and the Civil Engineer was faced in 1927 with the fact that virtually the whole of the down line of the former Midland & South Western Junction was in need of re-laying over the 13¾ miles between Cirencester and Andoversford Junction. In view of the levels of traffic over the route following the grouping, it was decided that the line could be singled, thus saving the re-laying of one track, although set against this was the cost of providing the two intermediate crossing loops and single-line signalling. Another saving was the 'economic system' of track maintenance on branch lines generally, the gangs being given long possessions at slack periods or overnight to enable one set of men to cover a greater mileage using trolleys rather than walking. With the further development of mechanically-propelled trolleys in 1928, it was found possible to extend the area of a single gang of men to cover the whole of the 13¼ miles between Rushey Platt Junction and Cirencester (Watermoor).

Tunnels came in for their share of attention. Moderately routine maintenance was fairly widespread over the seven years, but half a mile of the Severn Tunnel was strengthened by cement grouting, and a new ventilation plant was provided at Sudbrook to enable the tunnel to carry a greater number of trains. A major new tunnel, nearly 1,600 yards long, was constructed through the Malvern Hills at Colwall. It was built for a single track only, but of more generous proportions than the one it replaced, while the slightly less severe gradient adopted also contributed to the improvement in the working conditions for westbound trains.

As mentioned earlier, the Great Western came into the grouping with a number of new lines authorised but not built, and work progressed with some of these, such as the doubling of the Kingswinford Branch, and the building of a new 9½-mile single line from Himley to Wolverhampton. Elsewhere other goods lines were uprated to passenger standards, and new connections made for freight purposes. Numerous new halts were provided, together with some new stations, while there were various moves to increase the capacity of certain lines. Examples of these works were the construction of running loops between Bristol and Weston-super-Mare in 1925, and the doubling of one of the two remaining sections of single line in West Cornwall, west of St Erth. Interestingly, with the introduction in recent years of fixed formation trains capable of being driven from either end, the section from Long Rock to Penzance has been singled once more to provide space for a servicing shed for the InterCity 125 units. At the other end of the system, extensive alterations were put in hand in 1926 to increase the siding accommodation at Old Oak Common and to provide independent up and down carriage and wagon lines. All these improvements were to prove invaluable for handling the increased peak holiday traffic over the years that followed. On the Saturday before August Bank Holiday in 1926, the down 'Cornish Riviera' ran in no less than five portions, the 4–6–0 locomotives all working up to Paddington from Old Oak Common coupled together. The 'Torbay Express' on the same day ran in three parts. These eight sections of the Great Western's two premier trains conveyed a total of some 5,000 passengers, and provided a good indication of the passenger traffic the railway's new works were being geared to handle.

Signalling

Alongside these changes on the civil engineering side, there were, of necessity, improvements with the signalling arrangements. However, these were, on the whole, rather a case of 'more of the same' than any striking new developments. Some low-voltage and dynamo point machines and battery-operated signals were being installed at sites where they were particularly called for, together with electric-light fog repeaters on the Paddington–Old Oak Common section. Automatic colour lights were subsequently installed on the new carriage lines, while all four running tracks were track-circuited as far out as Acton West by 1929. On the other hand, the electrical power frame at Yarnton Junction was in the same year replaced by a mechanical locking one. The GWR system of Automatic Train Control, with ramps associated with each distant signal, had reached Oxford, High Wycombe and Swindon by the end of the 1920s. The double-wire system, unusual for this country, was installed at Park Junction near Newport to operate points up to 600 yards from the box, well beyond the 350-yard limit for ordinary push rods. The changed layout at Newport, opened in May 1926, enabled a new East box to be installed, replacing two previous ones, and a new electric power interlocking frame was used, although the running signals were semaphores. The box employed the route lever system, with the whole area being track-circuited.

There were, however, a number of interesting developments taking place with Great Western signalling, even if they did not represent any great technical steps forward. One of these was the change-over to yellow for distant signal arms and lights. Included under this heading was the installation of telephone equipment for railway operating purposes, the new Bristol goods station, for instance, being equipped with a twenty-line automatic switchboard. A carefully-staged test call from the Superintendent of the Line's office at Paddington was even carried out when the GPO's trans-Atlantic telephone service was inaugurated. There was also the need to standardise the GWR signalling system throughout the whole of the new group. A start was also made with the use of tubular signal posts and vitreous-enamelled arms. The new signalling associated with the Newton Abbot station rebuilding in 1926–27 was very traditional and still used wooden arms. The mechanical frame of over 200 levers in the new East box, however, probably provided some economies in operation.

Trains and Traffic

Having discussed the developments in the Great Western's motive power, rolling stock and track, we are now in a position to see how their train services changed during the period under discussion. With goods traffic bringing in well over half of the company's gross receipts during the 1920s, it is thus appropriate to consider initially the operation of the freight and mineral trains. It might come as a surprise to readers, but the *Great Western Railway Magazine*, in its review of 1924, referred to the fact that 'the standard of freight train working was well maintained, the miles per hour averaging between 6 and 7'. Such low speeds were by no means uncommon in steam days, but it was not long into the grouping before the *Magazine* launched its All-Line Goods Train Working Competition in April 1927. The results were discussed at length each month, and great interest was aroused. The vast majority of goods trains were unbraked, except for the guard's van, the services of which could be summoned specially by the driver using that unique Great Western feature fitted to each locomotive, the brake whistle. There was nevertheless an appreciable development of vacuum-braked trains, which totalled forty-one by the end of 1924. The most important of these overnight services were worked by the nine mixed-traffic 2–8–0 locomotives dating from just before the grouping. Certain forms of seasonal traffic were also handled by vacuum-braked trains. As well as the Channel Island produce already referred to, the Cornish broccoli traffic produced a considerable seasonal peak. This required the running of 348 wagon-loads in seven special trains on one particular day in the spring of 1926, to be followed next day by another 270. In 1929 some produce was even sent by train ferry to the Continent. The Worcestershire fruit season was another source of heavy seasonal traffic, 2,608 wagons being loaded at Evesham in August 1928, a record 214 being despatched from the one station in a single day. One of the Bulldog 4–4–0s had been named 'Pershore Plum' during the previous year for the same reason as Class 47s now sport names like 'Henry Ford'. Spring flowers from the Scilly Isles formed a further seasonal traffic, with up to forty tons in 7,500 boxes being put on trains at Penzance in a single day. Another similar source of traffic, this time a peripatetic one, concerned the various agricultural shows throughout the country. The Royal, held at Newport in 1927, for instance, required the transport of over 4,000 tons of material and exhibits, as well as 916 wagons of livestock in forty-two special trains, to a temporary depot there. There was a general speed-up of some of the more important long distance goods trains during the period, to help counter road competition. A record non-stop run of 145½ miles between Greenford and Shrewsbury was introduced on an overnight train in 1927, and by 1929 the Great Western was publishing its first *public* timetable for goods trains.

The Great Western also handled some notable one-off and out-of-gauge loads during the period, and the degree of trouble to which it went was amazing. One of the swiftest reactions ever was an out-of-gauge load sent 100 miles to London Docks one Sunday in 1925. Notification was only received on the previous afternoon, the Saturday, and some of the engineers' track occupations had to be cancelled or altered at little more than twelve hours' notice. Another unusual operation involved the lifting of a racing yacht out of the River Teign by a railway crane, and placing it on a wagon for transport to Brentford and ultimately Marseilles. Again it was an operation carried out at relatively short notice because of rough seas in the Channel. It was not solely traffic for the docks that involved

32. Castle class 4–6–0 no 4092 'Dunraven Castle' heads the down 'Torbay Pullman' past Ruscomb on 23 September 1929.

M. W. Earley Collection, National Railway Museum, York

unusual loads. In 1926 a sixteen-ton meter for a gas works, ten feet in diameter, was sent from South Lambeth to Exeter, and required no less than ten horses to collect it from the manufacturers on a special lorry.

Although the rates fixed for goods traffic were controlled by the new Railway Rates Tribunal, it was not until 1 January 1928 that the finally-agreed figures came into operation. There was a considerable simplification in the classification of goods, but the general effect was to stabilise rates at 160 per cent of those applied in 1914. It must be remembered that the railways were then still common carriers and had to take anything offered to them. Many exceptional rates for specific traffics had been granted by the railways over the years, and when they tried to raise these by the same proportion in 1927 a legal test case has been taken right through to the House of Lords by Tate & Lyle. Details of all rates, including exceptional cases, were kept at each station and were open to public inspection. Not only could other traders thus see what their competitors were paying, but so could the road hauliers. An interesting new facility was the extension of the Post Office's COD scheme to rail freight in 1928, and the limit of £40 was quite high enough to cover a wagon or two of coal in those days.

On the passenger side, the story of the 1920s was dominated from a publicity point of view by a handful of services. A number of these were specials, such as the trains already mentioned which were run in connection with ocean liners calling at Plymouth. The ordinary public time-table gave details of how these would be operated, and when 'an ordinary Fast Train' was not available, a special would be run for as few as thirty first-class or fifty third-class passengers. 'Friends of Ocean Passengers' were entitled to special rates for travel to Plymouth to meet those arriving and departing. Some fine running was put up by these specials, and great publicity made of the services generally. Another less usual special, run in connection with a party travelling by liner, was that used to convey the Australian cricket team from Paddington to Birkenhead in October 1926 on the first leg of their homeward journey. 'Windsor Castle' worked the special, which passed Birmingham without stopping in 106 minutes, with a maximum of 92 mph at Haddenham. The first stop at Shrewsbury, to change locomotives, was reached in 2 hours 40 minutes, and Woodside terminal in 3 hours 55 minutes. The overall running average worked out at 54.6 mph.

Since 1904 the flagship of the Great Western had been the 'Cornish Riviera' with its long-standing non-stop run from Paddington to Plymouth, and with the introduction of the Kings, the 1928 summer timing was cut to an even four hours. The publicity carefully referred to the fact that, although the train's overall speed was higher, the use of the more powerful locomotives meant the actual maximum speeds achieved were lower because of their superior uphill performance. Perhaps this was to pacify

any residual fears of passengers who might have heard of the derailment of the bogie of 'King George IV' at Midgham in August 1927. Fortunately the incident was without further consequence, but the bogies on the Kings were quickly redesigned to give increased springing flexibility and the trouble never recurred. The time-honoured practice of slipping coaches at Westbury, Taunton and Exeter in the down direction continued, lightening the load as the gradients increased in severity towards the West. So in the summer of 1928 the fourteen coaches that left Paddington had been reduced to six after Exeter. The through carriage to Newquay was detached at Plymouth, and the one for St Ives came off at St Erth, leaving only four to work right through to Penzance.

The 'Torbay Limited' was also running non-stop between Paddington and Torquay, and was joined in July 1929 by the 'Torbay Pullman Limited'. This marked the first regular use of Pullmans on the Great Western, and for that summer the train was run on Mondays and Fridays only. An additional round-trip on Saturdays was introduced in the autumn, but the train was not as fast as the ordinary 'Torbay Limited', which meant there was no speed advantage to help justify the 7s 6d (37½p) and 5s (25p) first class and third class supplements. A quarter of a century and a World War later, the supplements on the 'Tees Tyne Pullman' for the slightly longer journey from King's Cross to Darlington were still only 11s (55p) and 6s (30p), so the Pullman Car Company appeared to be charging passengers in 1929 somewhat highly for the privilege.

The actual date of the introduction of the 'Pullman' was 8 July, and this represented a red-letter day at Paddington. It was James Milne's first day as General Manager, and he was among those that saw the 'Riviera' off with its train of new stock, Collett ringing the bell on

33. Holiday crowds on no 1 platform at Paddington on 14 July 1928. The roof-board on the nearest coach reads 'Paddington & Aberystwyth for Carmarthen'. This stock would have formed the 10.20 from Paddington to Aberystwyth & Pwelleli, so that north of Birmingham the coaches to the former destination would have provided a reasonable connection to Carmarthen even if there was a quicker direct route from London.

'King George V' before it departed. The real fireworks, however, were to take place in the afternoon, when 'Launceston Castle' was to cut two minutes off the schedule of the inaugural run of the fastest start-to-stop train in the world. This was the 'Cheltenham Spa Express', more usually known by its unofficial title of the 'Cheltenham Flyer'. In 1923 the schedule for the 77.3 miles up from Swindon had been reduced to seventy-five minutes, corresponding to an average of 61.8 mph, but this was trimmed in 1929 by five minutes. The nine bogies of the inaugural train had been whisked up to London in sixty-eight minutes exactly, in spite of a signal check at Acton. It was a magnificent achievement even if it was to be well and truly beaten during the 1930s. On the Birmingham line, the Kings took over the principal trains, their extra power being used to increase the loadings. Even at the end of the 1930s the Great Western was content to retain two-hour bookings on that route. A notable introduction in 1924 was the standardisation of departure times from Paddington, a feature which we take very much for granted today.

Third-class fares had been fixed at 1½d (0.625p) per mile throughout the country, and these were confirmed by the Rates Tribunal in 1928. There were, however, a number of promotional fares too, introduced on the same basis by all the railway companies, the most notable being the day and half-day excursions. They utilised special trains, and attracted vast crowds on occasions. The first half-day excursion on the Great Western after World War I was in May 1925, and 3,500 passengers travelled to Weston-super-Mare from Paddington at a fare of 7s 6d (37½p). By mid-August the railway was handling no less than 25,000 of these excursionists on a single day, in fifty-one specials, over half of them travelling to Weston-super-Mare from various parts of the system. It was hardly surprising that the Deputy Chairman of the Great Western, Sir Ernest Palmer, was asked to open the new Winter Gardens there in the summer of 1927. Before this, however, the season ticket holders at the resort had in 1924 entertained the local railway staff to a complimentary dinner. Earlier that year nearly 40,000 passengers had arrived in Cardiff for the Wales versus Scotland rugby international, while in 1926 ninety-three special trains were run for the army manoeuvres on Salisbury Plain. Clearly, peak traffic of this sort required the provision of extra facilities in various places, which kept the Civil Engineer busy. It was not only the seaside that could be used to attract excursion passengers. Various very successful schemes were run, such as 'Educational' and 'Holiday Accommodation' excursions. Others included river trips and visits to cathedrals, liners or the theatre, while for the railway enthusiast there were the famous trips to Swindon Works to see the Kings being built, with locomotives of that class being used on the train itself. On the first occasion these trains ran, one of them managed an overall time of only 68¼ minutes for the 77¼ miles back to Paddington, everyone leaving the train feeling they had had good value for their 5s (25p). Nowadays it costs more to get to Royal Oak!

It was not just excursion traffic that increased in the late 1920s, as there was already a general move of the population out of London. Iver station was opened in 1924, and in the five years up to 1928 season ticket sales at twelve stations within forty miles of Paddington increased from 51,000 to 132,000.

Road Transport

The 1920s marked the emergence of the road transport industry, World War I having provided the impetus for the technical development of the vehicles which were then available for adoption by commercial interests generally. It is most interesting to note the railway's reactions to this new form of competition. At the time of the grouping the annual index to the *Great Western Railway Magazine* had no entries whatever under 'Roads' in any form, but by 1928 there were more than a dozen such references, by which time the Great Western had already established its own Road Transport Department. The main reason for this surge of interest was based on the old adage, 'if you can't beat them, join them', and the railways as a whole were anxious to ensure that they would be allowed to operate passenger and freight services by road in exactly the same way as their competitors.

As we saw in Chapter 1, the Great Western inaugurated the first railway-owned motor road service in the country back in 1903, even beating the capital city with the provision of such a facility. By the 1920s, road motors were replacing or supplementing horse-drawn delivery vehicles for freight cartage from the stations, but there was considerable doubt, even before the grouping, about what was the railways' legal position with such services. The Railways Act of 1921 had clarified the situation somewhat, but to the railways' positive exclusion, and the lobbying from 1926 to 1928 was all directed at getting them full freedom to participate in the new industry on a simple commercial basis, unfettered in any way compared with their competitors.

The road versus rail arguments are still going on sixty years later, but it is particularly interesting to read those that were being used in the 1920s to justify the new statutory powers the railways were seeking. The upkeep and improvement of the roads was largely at the expense of the parish ratepayers in those days, and there were numerous places where the

THE RAILWAY COMPANIES SEEK ROAD POWERS—

To obtain as ratepayers the same rights on the roads as other ratepayers

To secure a full measure of co-ordination between road and rail transport

To keep railway rates affecting the basic industries at the lowest possible level

British Rail Western Region

34. A 1928 poster seeking public support for the railways' campaign to obtain rights to transport goods and passengers by road.

railways were actually providing the biggest share of the rates, which were calculated on their passenger and freight receipts. The 1921 Act had guaranteed the railways a net revenue, and they argued that if they were to lose traffic to road competition, their transport charges would have to go up to compensate. (It is difficult to realise now how deeply-rooted was the suspicion amongst the public that the railways would abuse their virtual monopoly in land transport to set prohibitively high carriage rates, but the safeguards built into the Railways Act of 1921 are sufficient to remind us of the contemporary situation.) In the Parliamentary session of 1927/28, each of the grouping companies, as well as the Metropolitan Railway, submitted its own bill to obtain the rights it required, backing up its case with posters such as the one illustrated on p. 83. The outcome was ultimately successful in the case of the main-line companies, whose Acts received the Royal Assent in August 1928, although the ideas then germinating for a unified London Transport system resulted in the Metropolitan's being rejected. The Big Four were correspondingly restricted from operating in the London Traffic Area. It is against this background, therefore, that the Great Western's participation in the road transport scene in the 1920s must be viewed.

As we have already seen, the development of road cartage to and from railheads was already in progress, some of the vehicles, or their bodywork, being built at Swindon. The central maintenance depot at Slough was substantially enlarged in 1925, and in the following years various depots were provided with facilities for the bulk storage of petrol. The rural railhead distribution system was developed considerably, with road vehicles operating over a radius of twenty miles from a goods station. While these facilities were available for any consignee, they were primarily developed where regular services were required by particular suppliers. During the same period the Great Western was steadily taking over the local cartage services in numerous centres which had previously been operated by agents. Some quite large vehicles were among the 1,300 in use by the end of the 1920s, including three-axle Foden steam lorries. They were equipped with solid tyres, but the 1925 extensions at Slough had included a 'vulcanising plant for repairing damaged pneumatic tyres'. That year had seen the addition of eighty small fast buses with pneumatic tyres to the Company's stock. Another of the developments

in the late 1920s was the sugar beet trade, and although not serving the primary beet-growing areas, the Great Western invested considerably in systems to handle this important new crop. Initially the road cartage was to railheads, but after the passing of the 1928 Act it was possible for the railways to carry beet by road direct from farm to processing plant where appropriate. The start of the container business has already been noted, four different types being available with capacities ranging from 2½ to four tons. This development was again a general one covering all four main-line companies. As late as 1925 the Great Western's Road Transport Department was reporting that a larger complement of horses was necessary to handle the increased amount of short-range cartage, but nevertheless could claim a decrease of nearly 10 per cent on the overall cartage costs per ton compared with the previous year. Authorisation was given during 1928 to eliminate horses completely from the South Lambeth depot, but the system-wide change-over was to be very protracted, lasting until after nationalisation. The Great Western's last horse omnibus was, however, retired in 1924.

On the bus side, the Great Western had been active in the introduction of new feeder services from the early days of the grouping, one of the routes introduced in 1925 being between Wantage Road and Swindon, serving Wantage town itself, which enabled the independent road-side steam tramway to cease its passenger services. The west of England, in particular, saw considerable development of short-distance bus services, handling local market traffic as well as train passengers throughout the year, supplemented by visitors in the tourist season. There was provision at this stage for awkward trunks and other impedimenta to be carried on the roofs of the vehicles. The operators had to contend with considerable variations in traffic

35. One of the GWR's Maudslay buses outside Slough station in May 1928. The vehicle is equipped with electric and manual horns, as well as two different designs of light, but the former oil-lit ones appear to have been modified for electricity.

British Rail Western Region

during the course of each week, as well as the usual summer increase. Solid-tyred vehicles with twenty-eight seats were used in the early days, but were replaced on the busier routes in the later 1920s by somewhat larger pneumatically-tyred vehicles, which actually had brakes on all four wheels. In 1927, for example, the purchase of no less than seventy-five of these new 32-seaters was authorised. The company's omnibuses were also represented at the Commercial Motor Show of that year, amongst its nine exhibits at Olympia. Another development in 1927 was the introduction of the 'Land Cruises', providing passengers with the opportunity to make combined rail and road journeys through some of the more scenic parts of the country served by the Great Western. Finding uses for these vehicles in the winter was always a problem, but in October 1928 some of the fifteen-seater 'Land Cruise' armchair cars were put into service between Oxford and Cheltenham, to provide a road-rail link in competition to the rival all-road service to London. The Great Western always seemed to attach considerable importance to this particular route, its last-ever timetable in October 1947 still devoting the usual whole page to advertising the service.

After the passing of the Railway Road Powers

Act of 1928, the whole direction of development altered. Instead of introducing their own services, the railways tended to invest heavily in new companies, in conjunction with existing operators. In their first round, the Great Western's involvement covered four companies as shown in Table 7.

There was joint involvement with the Southern Railway in the case of the Devon General, and this cooperation went further as there was a second important west of England bus company, the Southern National, whose offices, like those of the Western National, and later the Royal Blue Express Services, were all to be at the same address in Queen Street, Exeter. The two National companies in the west of England adopted identical liveries as well as ordering identical new vehicles, many of them 'Bristols'. To the uninitiated, the areas served by the Southern and Western National were somewhat confusing. The Western National operated several routes that were well to the east of those worked by the Southern National, which had a monopoly of the North Devon services, well to the north of the Western National's territory. The answer was that the Southern National and Western National were tied into those particular areas predominantly served by the Southern and Great Western Railways respectively. The degree of integration between road and rail was remarkable, with the buses in most towns serving the railway stations directly. There was interavailability of tickets, too, in certain cases, but the railways were very careful to ensure that their associated bus companies did not compete too directly with their railway operations. To quote an example from the Southern National's area, the very frequent Barnstaple-Bideford services were symbiotic with the ribbon-development along the A39 road from Barnstaple to Instow that took place between the World Wars. It was clear that this service did not

Table 7   ROAD SERVICES IN THE WESTERN AREA

Name	Area of Operation	Comprising
Western National Omnibus Co. Ltd	Devon and Cornwall south of line drawn from Newquay through Okehampton to Exeter; also parts of Somerset, Gloucestershire, Dorset and Wilts.	GWR road services in Cornwall and Devon, Westbury and Stroud. National Omnibus and Transport Co's services in area defined. West Penwith Motor Co.
Western Welsh Omnibus Co Ltd	South Wales, south of a line drawn from Aberayron to Hereford.	All GWR services in South Wales and Monmouthshire. South Wales Commercial Motors Ltd. Lewis & James Ltd. Barretts, Ltd. Cridlands, Ltd. Trescillian Motors, Ltd.
Crosville Motor Services Ltd	North Wales, north of a line drawn from Aberayron to Hereford.	All GWR services in Wrexham. Oswestry, Corwen, Dolgelley, Pwllheli, and Aberystwyth areas. Wrexham and District Transport Co's services.
Devon General Omnibus & Touring Co Ltd	South Devon. Area bounded by line Dartmouth, Okehampton, Bampton, Sidmouth.	All Devon General, and Ashcrofts Paignton, services.

really abstract rail traffic that might use the intermediate station at Fremington. On the other hand, the bus services southward along the Taw Valley ran no further than Bishops Tawton, well short of the first railway station at Chapelton on the SR line to Exeter.

The railways did not, of course, control all the bus services throughout the country, and in 1929 they jointly started to put pressure on their tourist and ticket agencies to prevent the latter also representing the independent road operators. A circular letter was sent to all agencies, making it quite clear that such arrangements were only possible after special assent had been obtained. Permission would only be granted for combined rail-road journeys, the agencies' own tours or for road services that did not compete with the railways. Agencies were naturally encouraged to represent those road services being developed that were directly associated with the railway companies. As we will see in the second volume, the railways successfully applied exactly the same ploy with the rival air services during the 1930s.

Although the associated road companies were eventually to represent the Great Western's entire involvement in road passenger transport after the passing of the 1928 Act, its final independent fling took place that particular summer with the introduction of a motor service to the top of a mountain. I cannot do better than to quote from the report in the *Great Western Railway Magazine* for September 1928, which read as follows:

Motor Coach Trips to Summit of Plynlimmon

A regular omnibus service of a unique character was commenced on August 2nd, by the Great Western Railway, by which passengers are conveyed from Aberystwyth to the summit of Plynlimmon. The vehicle leaves Aberystwyth at 10 a.m. and runs via Devil's Bridge to the mountain top, leaving the beaten track for a distance of three miles, and travelling through unprepared territory over grass, heath, and bog.

Passengers are conveyed back about midday to Devil's Bridge, where time is allowed for lunch and a view of the Falls before returning to Aberystwyth by light railway through the picturesque Rheidol Valley.

The car is of an experimental design, being a Morris six-wheeler with eight speeds and of a type which is in considerable use in the Army. The body of the car is open and passengers are equipped with large aprons to protect them from the mountain mists which are often encountered during the journey up the mountain. It has not been possible to provide a hood or any other cover to the vehicle owing to the very high winds which are encountered at the top of the mountain. The charabanc body gives an opportunity of seeing the magnificent views which are obtainable on the trip. The car is controlled entirely by the engine, the brakes only being required in cases of emergency.

This is the first excursion of its kind attempted in England, and possibly in the world, and the interest shown by the public in the undertaking would lead one to think that it will be a forerunner of many similar expeditions, which would throw open to the travelling public beauty spots which hitherto have only been accessible to the hardy mountaineer.

Accompanying the account was a whole-page photograph showing the vehicle on a ferociously-steep hillside covered with grass and bushes. The over-wide tyres on the twin rear axles could be fitted with the tracks carried on the running board, while a stout spade was strapped vertically to the nearside panelling of

36. In October 1928, near Northleach in the Cotswolds, two of the fifteen-seater armchair cars used for the 'Land Cruises' during the summer meet on the first day of the GWR's Oxford–Cheltenham service.

the box-like body which tapered outwards towards the top. The passengers were clearly taking their pleasures seriously, but one cannot help wondering about their headgear. The lady with a cloche hat would probably not be in too much difficulty with the winds at the summit, but her travelling companion in a pill-box hat would clearly have a problem, as would the men with their trilbys, not to mention the driver and his peaked cap. The return fare for this unique journey from Aberystwyth was 7s 6d (62½p), and represented quite a premium over the Vale of Rheidol return fare, which, at the usual 1½d (.625p) per mile, came to less than half that for the special trip. The following year the vehicle's operations were extended on certain days of the week to the Birmingham City reservoirs in the Elan Valley, reached by the Old Roman Road over the mountains. All in all, a remarkable ending to the quarter of a century of the Great Western Railway's pioneering efforts in the field of passenger travel by road.

Marine Activities

As with most of the Great Western Railway's engineering activities, the years immediately following the grouping were to see great improvements in their maritime activities. In typical Great Western style, a party of directors and principal officers embarked on the 'St Andrew' at Portland in July 1923 and cruised to Guernsey and Jersey to meet the important residents of the Channel Islands. An immediate result was the appearance of the first turbine-powered steamers for the service, the 'St Julien' and the 'St Helier', the former making her first passenger crossing in May 1925. They replaced the 'Ibex' and 'Reindeer', which, as already noted, dated back to 1891 and 1897 respectively. In size they were appreciably larger than any previous vessel on their Channel Islands services, and had a speed of nineteen knots. Originally built with twin funnels, the second one, a dummy, was removed in 1928 to cut down on the effects of windage when manoeuvring in the confines of the harbours at each end. Both returned to railway service after World War II, being sold for breaking up in 1960 ('St Helier') and 1961 ('St Julien'). There was a striking oil painting by Charles Pears in the corridor near the General Manager's office at Paddington showing the 'St Helier' returning with evacuated troops from Dunkirk in 1940, the night-time view showing the ship in silhouette against the burning port installations. From the passengers' points of view they had many improved facilities, and the provision of sleeping berths in the dining saloons was abolished. They also carried cargo and other forms of traffic, and on one crossing I made after nationalisation racing pigeons were released in mid-channel from hampers stacked on the hatch covers of the rear hold.

In addition to these new passenger vessels, the Great Western also placed two new cargo vessels in service in 1925. These were the 'Roebuck' and 'Sambur', oil-fired like the larger ships, but provided with triple-expansion engines which were adequate for the lower speeds required. They replaced the 'Lynx' and 'Gazelle' which dated back to 1889. This was modernisation with a vengeance, four ships with an aggregate age of 134 years being replaced in a single year by the same number of improved vessels. The Channel Islands, of course, provided a lot of perishable produce for the mainland, and the Great Western was anxious to retain its share of the business, including the rail haul from Weymouth to London and elsewhere. Flowers in the spring were followed by the early potatoes; then came the two tomato seasons. Guernsey, traditionally growing its tomatoes under glass, was first on the market, while those in Jersey were planted out in the fields after the potatoes had been lifted. Thousands of boxes or trays would be craned aboard each morning in St Helier during each crop's season, the produce having been sorted and prepared for transport in the various warehouses close to the harbour. On one day in September 1926 no less than 94,394 packages of tomatoes from the islands were handled at Weymouth and in the following year half the Jersey new potato crop of 55,000 tons was handled by the railway companies' ships, the Southern and GWR vessels running on alternate days.

At the Weymouth end the transport arrangements were not too convenient from the railway's point of view, there being a one-mile

37. The 'St Julien' as built in 1925 for the Weymouth Channel Islands service with two funnels. The second, dummy one was removed three years later to improve her handling in high winds.

tramway to connect the main line just north of Weymouth station with the landing stage at the harbour. This largely ran along the quays and through the streets, and in later years trains even had to comply with a 'Halt at Major Road Ahead' sign. Not only had all trains to be preceded by a member of the railway staff on foot (who was permitted, though, according to the original regulations, to ride on the 'front buffer plank'), but the sharp curvature of the tramway required some unique operating practices. Bogie stock had to have the screw coup-lings replaced by extra-long three-link loose ones, which naturally also involved the discon-nection of the gangways and the locking of their doors. Even so, not all types of passenger stock were permitted to operate over the tramway, and those so authorised had a small cast iron plate on each end marked with the initials W Q and an overall diagonal cross. The articulated sets introduced in 1925 were used with some advantage on the tramway, as on them the coupling and uncoupling was confined to the non-articulated ends of the coaches. There were also weight restrictions on the tramway, and some unusual locomotives were used. At the time of the grouping the trains were in the hands of two 0–6–0 tanks of Bristol & Exeter origin, supplemented by a 0–6–0 saddle-tank which came from the Hook Norton Ironstone Partnership. They were followed in the late 1920s by a pair of six-coupled saddle tanks from the Burry Port & Gwendraeth Valleys Railway, while in the 1930s another relic from the Cornwall Minerals Railways was sent for use on the line. Congestion at peak times was frequent, and in order to carry out the shunting in the restricted space available it was standard practice to use a steel cable so that the locomotive could move a string of wagons (up to forty-five at times) on the next track. Its use was vital on one siding over which locomotives were prohibited. The whole tramway was an operator's nightmare, but once on the main line the boat trains were handled with despatch, a larger turntable being installed at Weymouth in 1925 to permit the use of the Castles. On the London run, eleven-coach boat trains were worked over the 154½ miles in three hours, an average of 51½ mph, which included the 1 in 50 gradients that faced trains in both directions between Yeovil and Weymouth.

The oil firing that had been adopted on the 1925 vessels was to prove invaluable during the coal strike of the following year, and the 'St Helier' and 'St Julien' were both put on to the winter service between Fishguard and Rosslare, while for several weeks the oil-fired ships from Weymouth provided the only services to and from the Channel Islands for mails and passengers.

Further West, at Plymouth, a new passenger tender, the 'Sir John Hawkins', the largest of the fleet, was put into service in July 1929, to help handle the growing trans-Atlantic traffic. She joined the 1908 twins, 'Sir Francis Drake' and 'Sir Walter Raleigh,' together with the older vessel 'Sir Richard Grenville', which dated from 1891. All were coal-fired and had considerable work to perform, there being no less than 788

calls by liners in 1929. There were at times as many as four visits in a single day.

When it came to the profitability of the Great Western's shipping fleet, the picture is a surprising one. In 1923 expenditure was 16 per cent greater than receipts, and this margin was to rise to a peak of 43 per cent two years later, when the actual deficit was £116,000. That particular year was, however, very much the worst of a bad patch; thereafter the annual loss fell back to about its earlier level, although, by the end of the period under review, the deficit was cut to a mere £1,200 in 1929. The pattern then was for the Channel Islands services to be run daily during the summer, with daytime passages in each direction. During the winter the service was cut to alternate days and the southbound sailings were overnight. There were no such drastic seasonal changes with the services from Fishguard to Rosslare and Waterford, the sea crossings always being overnight.

Hotels, Refreshment Rooms and Restaurant Cars

The first seven years of the grouping were active ones for the department feeding the Great Western's passengers, and accommodating them in its hotels. There is perhaps no more rapidly changing facet of railway service than the provision of food and drink, and then, as now, the availability of facilities of different sorts was being constantly tailored to the demands of the public. Throughout the period the Great Western managed to make a surplus of 9 to 14 per cent on its annual turnover of some £600,000, providing a marked constrast to the present-day costs of providing on-train catering. However, there are quite distinct limits to the productivity increases that can be achieved with the service of meals in dining rooms whether mobile or static,

38. The Fishguard Bay Hotel in July 1929.

and inevitably the wages of those who wait at table rise in general sympathy with those in industry, where mechanisation and automation can bring vastly increased productivity.

The whole tempo of travel was, however, much slower in the 1920s than today, and 1928 saw the introduction of restaurant car services over journeys as short as the sixty-three miles between Oxford and Paddington. Tea and dinner would be served on Ocean Liner specials between Plymouth and Paddington, the most notable instance being when 375 members of the

American Hotels Association were served by the eight cars provided on the two trains involved. A few days later the party was taken by special to Oxford and Stratford-upon-Avon, the members being presented with tins of chocolate biscuits by girls from Huntley and Palmers, while the train halted at Reading. The total meals served each year in the cars rose by about 20 per cent during the period, to a total of 1½ million. The latest developments in food quality were carefully watched, 'certified' milk being used from 1926 onwards, while a banana-ripening room was built at Bristol in the same year to enable the fruit to be distributed to trains and refreshment rooms at its best.

There was a gradual take-over of some of the independently-operated station refreshment rooms until over eighty were being directly managed. There were proper dining rooms in many of the larger stations, and when new buildings were constructed the opportunity was taken to provide quite extensive facilities. A 'handsome cafe and restaurant, with dance floor' was provided in the new station building at Newton Abbot, following on from the one at Aberystwyth in the previous year, where 'a spring floor for dancing has been laid, and dances, held almost weekly during the past season, were patronised by holidaymakers and residents of the town'. Perhaps more remarkable still, the restaurant facilities at Swindon included a masonic temple.

On the hotels side, the fortunes of the Royal Station Hotel at Paddington seem to have been somewhat fickle, in spite of the construction of numerous additional bathrooms. Extra business was attracted by the British Empire Exhibition of 1924, but the subsequent industrial difficulties seem to have affected it more than the company's other hotels. The kitchen however won a gold medal at the Universal Cookery and Food Exhibition at Olympia in 1928 for a dinner of six courses for six people. On the same occasion the 'cook' of the Cheltenham restaurant car was awarded a bronze medal for 'a typical English dish'. Down at St Ives business at the Tregenna Castle Hotel was booming after the 1923 extension, so much so that a further new wing was completed in 1929. In spite of their new nine-hole golf course, they were still only second best to the Manor House Hotel at Moretonhampstead which was bought and converted by the GWR in that year. Its eighteen-hole course was featured on television as late as the 1980s during the last few years of its ownership by British Transport Hotels. The home farm at the Tregenna Castle, however, was noted for its prize-winning cattle at West of England shows. The special attraction for sporting visitors to the remaining country hotel, the Fishguard Bay, was fishing, which had eight miles of its own water carefully restocked with trout in the spring of 1925. As with so many of its other operations, the Great Western's hotel business was conducted in style.

Staff

Between 1924 and 1929 the total staff on the Great Western Railway fell from 117,000 to 106,000, although the figure was actually to rise again in the following year. As we have already seen, the company was at great pains to foster loyalty, safety and efficiency amongst its employees. The General Manager was constantly out and about throughout the system, presenting awards of one sort or another to the various staff organisations, and also entertained his staff at an annual garden party at his own residence, Calcot Park, Reading. Ambulance competitions are still a well-established feature of the railway scene, but activities of the Social and Educational Union were widespread in the 1920s. In 1926, for instance, the prize choirs and gold medallist of that year's music festival provided a seventy-minute programme for the British Broadcasting Company's Birmingham studio. Other competitions were held for horticulture and public speaking, while the GWR Swindon Mechanics' Institution included amateur theatricals in its activities. The All Line Goods Train Competition has already been mentioned, and this was later complemented by a Passenger Train Punctuality competition. On the athletics side, too, there was great activity, with all-line bowls,

39. A GWR driver climbs aboard Saint 4–6–0 no 2935 'Caynham Court' at Paddington. In 1931 this locomotive was rebuilt with rotary cam poppet valve gear. Although no other GWR locomotive was so equipped, 'Caynham Court' remained at work until the end of 1948.

cricket and tennis competitions during the summers, which also saw the railway companies at their Territorial Army camps. Another notable institution was the Lecture and Debating Society, which throughout the years was a forum for the discussion of technical and other matters. The 1929–30 season for the London society for instance, included papers on 'Changing from screw couplers on the Japanese Railways', and 'A Channel Tunnel. Is it desirable?'

At the railway town of Swindon the company's paternalism was at its most extensive. A major extension to the hospital was opened in 1929, and the welfare institutions included swimming baths which were also used by school children by arrangement with the local authorities. Elsewhere, however, the company was active in assisting its employees with the formation of Public Utility Housing Societies. These organisations were able to obtain various government and local authority subsidies, and garden villages were constructed in several centres. Over 800 houses were built or under construc-

40. A retirement picture at Paddington in May 1926. Mr Tom Willie left the railway after 50 years' service, and posed with (left to right) Mr N P Mansfield, the Station Master at Paddington, Mr H R Campfield, the Divisional Superintendent, and Mr Tom Gooding, the head guard of the 'Cornish Riviera Express'.

tion in 1927, with the assistance of loans from the railway amounting to over £340,000. The system gave security of tenure to those living on the estates, and at the same time enabled tenants to exchange houses if they were moved on company business.

The Results

The Great Western Railway was a statutory company, and had, at the end of each year, either to finish with a profit or at least to make ends meet. As we have seen, the seven years following the grouping were not the best economically for the country, but the Great Western was nevertheless able to maintain a reasonable annual net income, as shown in Table 8. The effect of the coal and general strikes in 1926 is most marked, but, apart from that year, its annual net income was in the range of £5.8m to 7.1m. There was an additional factor that contributed to the results in 1928 and 1929. 'In view of the conditions obtaining in the Railway Industry', agreement was reached with the unions that a 2½ per cent reduction would be made from the gross amount of wages and salaries throughout. By comparison with the LMS figures, the Great Western would have benefited by some

£175,000 in 1928 and £470,000 in the following year. Overall this represented about 7 per cent of the total net income for 1929. The investor largely judges the success of a company by its dividends, so Table 9 compares the performance of the GWR with the other main-line companies, and the bank rate. It will be seen that, throughout, the Great Western was declaring a higher dividend on its ordinary stock than any other company, its nearest rival being the LMS, which actually managed to equal the Great Western figure for the strike-torn year of 1926. Indeed, in many years most of the other companies' dividends showed no improvement on the bank rate.

So, as we leave the 1920s, the fortunes of the Great Western appear to be well on the ascendant, with receipts and income moving upwards once more. Various government measures had also been announced to help the railways generally, ranging from the relief of rates to the Development (Loan Guarantees and Grants) Act of 1929. This was to result in many notable improvements in the years to follow, including the Westbury and Frome cut-offs, which helped speed the trains to the West of England.. So, as the operators of the fastest railway train in the world, the Great Western was well poised to move into the 1930s, but its fortunes in the first few years of that decade were to be over-shadowed by the Great Depression, sparked off by the Wall Street crash of October 1929, which was to have a significant effect on most British commercial enterprises.

Table 8 GREAT WESTERN RAILWAY
FINANCIAL RESULTS 1923–1929

Year	Gross receipts (£'000)	Revenue expenditure (£'000)	Total net income (£'000)
1923	36 723	29 779	6 945
1924	36 408	30 340	6 069
1925	35 242	29 458	5 784
1926	29 915	26 814	3 100
1927	37 079	30 016	7 063
1928	35 528	29 408	6 119
1929	36 184	29 209	6 975

Source: GWR Company Accounts

Table 9 RAILWAY DIVIDENDS AND BANK RATE

	Dividends on ordinary Shares (per cent)						
	GWR	LMS	LNER		SR		Bank rate
Year			Preferred	Deferred	Preferred	Deferred	
1923	8	7	5	2½	5	3½	3–4
1924	7½	7	5	2½	5	3½	4
1925	7	6	5	1	5	3½	4–5
1926	3	3	⅛	—	5	1¼	5
1927	7	4¾	⅜	—	5	2	5–4½
1928	5	3½	¼	—	5	2	4½
1929	7½	4½	3	—	5	2½	4½–6

Source: LMS Handbook of Statistics 1930–31

Index

Index